THINGS BEYOND
OUR CONTROL

a play

by

Jesse Kellerman

SAMUEL FRENCH, INC.

45 West 25th Street   7623 Sunset Boulevard
NEW YORK 10010   HOLLYWOOD 90046
LONDON   *TORONTO*

ISBN 0 573 60295 6   Printed in U.S.A.   #22276

IMPORTANT BILLING AND CREDIT REQUIREMENTS

All producers of *THINGS BEYOND OUR CONTROL must* give credit to the Author of the Play in all programs distributed in connection with performances of the Play and in all instances in which the title of the Play appears for purposes of advertising, publicizing or otherwise exploiting the Play and/or a production. The name of the Author *must* appear on a separate line on which no other name appears, immediately following the title, and *must* appear in size of type not less than fifty percent the size of the title type.

Characters

(in order of appearance)

ROBERTA, 43

MIRANDA, mid-30s, an airline employee

THE AMAZING TARQUIN, 65, a magician

GLEN, 46

DEWEY, 17, Glen's son

RICHIE, 44, a cab driver

OPAL, 27, a waitress

STEIN, 29, a medical resident

A WAITER, played by the same actor who plays Dewey

Setting

Various locations around Dallas, Texas.

Time

The present.

Act I

Scene 1

(A gate at Dallas-Ft. Worth airport. The LED display reads FL # 613 LONDON DEP 11:15 PM. A shiny bullet trash can stage right, against a gray carpet-covered pillar. The can is overflowing. Through a large window stage left we see pounding rain; streaks of lightning illuminate the night sky. MIRANDA, mid-30s, is behind the desk, wearing an airline uniform. She is arguing with ROBER-TA, 43, a thin, jittery woman in a business suit.)

MIRANDA.	ROBERTA.
I'm sorry, it's company policy.	But I need to get there, you understand?

MIRANDA. Ma'am? It's company policy.

ROBERTA. That is *not* company policy.

MIRANDA. It is, it's company--

ROBERTA. *(Overlapping with "it's company...")* Then it's a *bad* policy.

MIRANDA. I'm very sorry about that, ma'am, but there's nothing I can--

ROBERTA. *(Pointing out the window.)* The plane is right there! I can see it!

5

MIRANDA. I know, ma'am, but--

(ROBERTA points to the LED display.)

ROBERTA. Look! That says 11:15! It's 11:07!

MIRANDA. It says in the ticket contract that--

ROBERTA. *(Overlapping with "contract...")* You're telling me the plane's going to sit there for eight minutes while I watch?

MIRANDA. Ma'am, I'd love nothing more than to put you on the plane, but--

ROBERTA. *Bull*shit!

MIRANDA. Talking like that is not--

ROBERTA. *The plane is still there!*

MIRANDA. It's company--

ROBERTA. Don't tell me it's company policy! It's company policy to leave passengers behind?

MIRANDA. Ma'am, if you don't calm down, I'm going--

ROBERTA. *(Overlapping with "calm down...")* I want to speak to a manager.

MIRANDA. I *am* a manager.

ROBERTA. Then I want to speak to your manager.

MIRANDA. Ma'am, I'm going to call security.

ROBERTA. There is a meeting in London that I am supposed to be at. That I *need* to be at.

MIRANDA. *(Overlapping with "that I need to be...")* I'm perfectly happy to try and accomodate you tomorrow morning, if you'd just--

ROBERTA. I am going to write a letter.

MIRANDA. Ma'am. I am trying to help you.

ROBERTA. Then let me on the goddamned plane!

MIRANDA. I can't.

ROBERTA. WHY NOT!

MIRANDA. It's company policy that--

ROBERTA. *(Overlapping with "that")* Oh Christ...

MIRANDA. --that passengers must arrive at the gate ten minutes before departure--

ROBERTA. I *was--*

MIRANDA. --*twenty* minutes before an international flight. It's on your ticket. Twenty minutes before departure we close the doors, and once they are closed we are not allowed to reopen them. If you arrive any later than that, your seat is subject to forfeiture.

ROBERTA. This is theft...

MIRANDA. Your seat was given away already, ma'am. Even if the plane was not closed--*(She points out the window.)*--and even if the plane was *not* already moving--

ROBERTA. Oh, shit...!

(ROBERTA runs to the window and watches the plane pull away.)

MIRANDA.	ROBERTA.
--I would not be able to give you your seat, because your seat is already given away. There's someone else there. Now, I can accomodate you...	*(Slowly)* Shit. Shit. Shit. Shit. Shit. Shit. Shit. Shit. Shit. Shit. Shit...

MIRANDA....tomorrow. There is a flight I can get you on that will have you in London at...

ROBERTA. Oh, shit...

MIRANDA. ...ten AM Thursday. Would you like me to arrange that? *(ROBERTA wanders toward a seat, slumps in it. Small pause.)* Ma'am? Would you like me to arrange that?

(Small pause.)

ROBERTA. What?

MIRANDA. There's a flight tomorrow that will--

ROBERTA. I don't have anywhere to stay tonight.

(Small pause.)

MIRANDA. We might be able to accomodate you with a hotel tonight, if you're interested. *(Small pause.)* Would you like me to put

you on the flight tomorrow? *(Small pause. ROBERTA nods.)* All right.
Let me see what I can do about a hotel.

(She exits. ROBERTA stares out the window. Blackout.)

Scene 2

*(A street corner. THE AMAZING TARQUIN, 65, a magician, holds a
flaming torch. He wears a tight purple outfit and a cape.)*

THE AMAZING TARQUIN. The origins of beauty, ladies and gentlemen, are so often misunderstood. Whence comes the delightful if not
from the grotesque? For it is truly a blind man who sees only in cowshit
something brown, wet, inchoate, and reprehensible. If not for fertilizer,
where would we get tomatoes? Or potatoes? Or tomahtoes? Or potah-
toes? For diversity is the spice of life, and if life isn't spicy, Rolaids goes
out of business. And since I own nine thousand shares of Pfizer, I am
vehemently opposed to that. *(He waves the torch around.)* Watch the
fire, ladies and gentlemen, watch it! Don't take your eyes off it! If you
do I'll pull a fast one on you. I might pull one anyway. Or I might *get*
pulled. Thank god there's no hooks on street corners. *(He looks around.)*
Or *are* there? Dallas is a strange place, I gotta admit it. Tough crowds.
Maybe hooks abound, and I don't know it. Hooks on every corner,
designed especially to remove poor street performers with large stock
portfolios, men just like me. *(He waves the torch.)* Are you watching,
ladies and gentlemen? Are you? Watch closely! Appearances are
deceiving. Some might contend that they *can* be deceiving, but I would
argue, *nay.* They are seldom anything but. *(He waves the torch.)* Ladies
and gentlemen! I hope you're watching! And I hope you're walleting!
Wallets or watches, it's all the same to me, just keep your *eyes* on my
dis*guise* and I'll sup*plies* the grand sur*prise* that will en*tize* you to be
nize and give me each a little *prize.* Watch the fire, watch it, watch what
happens, and then dig deep in your Texas-sized pocketbooks, because

remember, ladies and gentlemen, beauty may come from unexpected places, but it *never* comes for free. *(He waves the torch.)* From trash comes fire, from fire comes smoke, from smoke come clouds, from clouds comes water, from water comes life, from life comes beauty, so don't *ever* question the purpose of Dallas!

(He snaps the torch. It turns into a bouquet of flowers. He smiles. Blackout.)

Scene 3

(A hotel room. ROBERTA is taking off her shoes. A soft knock at the door. ROBERTA looks at the digital clock: it is 1:15 in the morning. She frowns, gets up, looks through the eyehole. After a small pause, she opens the door. Standing there is MIRANDA. She is holding a pie tray covered in foil.)

MIRANDA. I've been very upset thinking about you. I'm so sorry about you missing your flight, and you looked so sad when I left, and I wished there was something I could do. But it was company policy. I told you that. I wish I wasn't, but I'm just an employee. *(Small pause.)* May I come in? *(Small pause. ROBERTA nods. She steps aside to allow MIRANDA in. MIRANDA places the pie on the nightstand and sits on the bed. ROBERTA stares at her.)* I brought you a pie.

(Small pause.)

ROBERTA. Thank you.
MIRANDA. It's peach. It's no big deal. I live near the airport.
ROBERTA. Thank you.
MIRANDA. You're welcome.

(Small pause.)

ROBERTA. I...I don't know if I'm going to eat it now.
MIRANDA. That's okay.
ROBERTA. I'm not...very hungry.
MIRANDA. Okay.
ROBERTA. But I'll take some and save it for tomorrow.
MIRANDA. For the plane ride.
ROBERTA. Yes. I don't mind airline food, but...
MIRANDA. It's terrible.

(ROBERTA laughs.)

ROBERTA. It's not so bad.
MIRANDA. Don't hold back for my sake, I don't cook it.
ROBERTA. All right, it's terrible.
MIRANDA. It's the second worst part of my job. The worst part is when I have to say no to people.

(Small pause.)

ROBERTA. What's the best part?
MIRANDA. Cheap travel. It's not quite free, but it's almost free.
ROBERTA. That must be nice.
MIRANDA. It is. *(She looks around.)* You need something to put the pie in.
ROBERTA. Oh. Hang on. *(She gets up, goes to the bathroom, returns with two plastic cups wrapped in plastic.)* I never used these before...*(She goes to the pie and peels back the foil.)* This smells delicious.
MIRANDA. Thank you.
ROBERTA. I'm not sure how to...

(She is trying to scoop the pie into the plastic cups, with little success.)

MIRANDA. Here. *(MIRANDA produces a knife. ROBERTA jumps back. Pause.)* It's to cut the pie with.

(Small pause.)

> ROBERTA. Sorry. *(Small pause.)* I'm sorry, that was very rude.
> MIRANDA. It's okay.
> ROBERTA. I mean, after you brought this all the way over.

(MIRANDA starts cutting the pie.)

> MIRANDA. It's no big deal, I live near the airport...

(She scoops some pie into one of the cups.)

> ROBERTA. This isn't going to be a very efficient way to travel, I
can tell already. It's going to get all over the place.
> MIRANDA. You can put the foil over the top.
> ROBERTA. That's a good idea.
> MIRANDA. There's nothing to worry about.
> ROBERTA. There's always something to worry about...that looks
really good.
> MIRANDA. Have a piece.
> ROBERTA. I can't.
> MIRANDA. Just take some.
> ROBERTA. I don't have a fork.
> MIRANDA. Just--here.

*(She takes a piece of pie between her fingers and offers it to ROBER-
TA.)*

> ROBERTA. No thanks.
> MIRANDA. What's the matter.
> ROBERTA. I prefer to eat with utensils.

(Small pause.)

> MIRANDA. You won't take it because I touched it?

ROBERTA. No, I--
MIRANDA. Then take it.
ROBERTA. I can't.

(Small pause. MIRANDA eats the piece herself.)

MIRANDA. I'm fine. I'm healthy. *(She sticks out her tongue.)* See?
ROBERTA. I see.
MIRANDA. Then you try it.
ROBERTA. I don't like to eat with my hands.
      MIRANDA. I'm not trying to be presumptuous, but your worries
seem out of order. I made this pie in my own home. You don't know
what's in it. You'd take a gift cooked by a stranger but you won't take a
piece with your hands? *(Small pause. ROBERTA is silent.)* All right.
*(MIRANDA goes back to scooping pie, now into the second cup. After a
pause, ROBERTA comes over to the pie, sticks her hand in, grabs a
piece and eats it. MIRANDA smiles at her.)* How does it taste?

(ROBERTA chews, swallows.)

ROBERTA. It's...delicious. *(She looks at her hands.)* I'm a mess.

(She starts toward the bathroom.)

MIRANDA. Wait a minute.
ROBERTA. I need a towel.
MIRANDA. Here.

*(She pulls the bedspread up, and offers it to ROBERTA, who does not
move. Small pause.)*

ROBERTA. I need a towel.

*(She exits to the bathroom. MIRANDA stares after her. A moment later,
ROBERTA returns, wiping her hands on a small towel.)*

MIRANDA. Better? *(ROBERTA nods.)* Okay. *(She takes the foil off the pie, starts wrapping the cups.)* Are you going to be okay tomorrow at your meeting?

ROBERTA. What?

MIRANDA. You're going to a meeting?

ROBERTA. ...yes.

MIRANDA. You'll make it on time?

ROBERTA. No. *(Small pause.)* I might lose my job.

(Small pause.)

MIRANDA. I'm sorry.

ROBERTA. It's...*(Small pause.)* It's really not that important.

MIRANDA. It isn't?

(Small pause.)

ROBERTA. No.

MIRANDA. Still. I wish I could have done something about getting you on the plane.

ROBERTA. It's not your fault. I was late. *(Small pause.)* The cabbie hit a guy on a bike.

(Small pause.)

MIRANDA. Oh my god.

ROBERTA. I...I know.

(Small pause.)

MIRANDA. Was he all right?

(Small pause.)

ROBERTA. I don't know.

MIRANDA. What...? *(Small pause.)* Oh. *(Small pause.)* You don't know? *(Small pause. ROBERTA shakes her head.)* Oh my god.

ROBERTA. I...I didn't...*(Small pause.)* He looked all right.

MIRANDA. But you don't know.

ROBERTA. No.

(Small pause.)

MIRANDA. The cabbie--?

ROBERTA. He didn't want to stop. Either.

(Small pause.)

MIRANDA. He didn't...?

ROBERTA. No. *(Small pause.)* He looked all right. He was...wearing a blue shirt. It had a flag on it. *(Small pause.)* I think he looked all right. *(Small pause.)* But I don't know. *(Small pause.)* I'm getting on a plane tomorrow.

(Small pause. Slowly, MIRANDA nods.)

MIRANDA. Yes.

ROBERTA. I'm sure he's all right.

MIRANDA. I hope so.

ROBERTA. So do I. *(Small pause.)* I'll...I'll find out. About him. When I get back, the first thing I'm doing is going, and...calling up... *(Small pause.)* I don't know. I'll call him up. *(Small pause. MIRANDA nods.)* I'll make sure he's okay. *(Pause.)* I feel like shit. *(Small pause. She starts to cry. After a pause, MIRANDA comes to her and embraces her. Crying.)* I'm hungry.

(MIRANDA goes to the pie, brings it to ROBERTA, who sits on the bed.)

MIRANDA. I'm sorry I don't have a fork.

ROBERTA. It's okay.

MIRANDA. You can take some.

(Small pause. ROBERTA looks up at MIRANDA.)

ROBERTA. Feed me.

(Small pause. MIRANDA looks at ROBERTA, then at the pie. MIRAN-DA reaches in and takes some pie in her hand. She offers it to ROBERTA, who eats from her hand. After ROBERTA is done eating, she still holds MIRANDA's hand. MIRANDA reaches back and puts the pie on the nightstand. She kneels down in front of ROBER-TA and kisses her hand. She holds ROBERTA's hand and looks into her eyes. Then MIRANDA reaches for the buttons on ROBERTA's blouse. She undoes several of them, then pulls ROBERTA's blouse open. MIRANDA kisses ROBERTA's chest. ROBERTA begins again to cry quietly. MIRANDA stretches up and kisses ROBERTA on the lips. Blackout.)

Scene 4

(An apartment. There is a bicycle helmet on the sofa. The front door opens and DEWEY, 17, enters. He is very banged up. His face is covered in scratches. His shirt--blue with a US flag on it--is torn, and his elbow is bleeding; ditto his pants at the knees. His expression is dazed, and his gait is uneven. To be accurate, he looks as though he has been hit by a car. He spots the helmet. From offstage his father, GLEN, calls. As he talks, DEWEY stares at the helmet.)

GLEN. (O.S.) Dewey? You're late. I ate already. If you want something you have to go heat it up. There's peas in the fridge. I made a casserole. It's mostly tuna but it's got all sorts of things in it. Or else it wouldn't be a casserole, it'd be baked alaska with tuna. There's also peach pie. I was considerate enough to get dessert. Dewey? Go on into the kitchen and have some dinner. *(As he continues, DEWEY steps toward the helmet, reaches out to pick it up. Halfway there, however, he wobbles, dizzy. He straightens and up tries to steady himself.)* Honest to god, Dewey, you're lucky I couldn't sleep. Else how'd you know about the stuff in the fridge. You'da gotten no dinner. What the hell are you doing, coming in at one in the morning? If you're off being with girls in your class, Dewey, my advice to you is that you use a prophy-lactic. *(Slowly, painfully, DEWEY bends and reaches for the helmet.)* If that is what you're doing, then I commend you all the more. You get two commendations: one for upholding the family name, and the other for using your head. I swear, if you inherited anything from me it was not your brains. Cause you got some. *(DEWEY manages to pick up the helmet.)* I wish to god I could sleep. I have to get up in three hours. I'm working straight through, two shifts straight, so you're on your own for dinner tonight, or tomorrow night, or whatever the hell it is, I don't know, I'm tired. Take care of it, you're on your own. You have my per-mission to bring in some take out. You don't have my explicit permis-sion to bring home cheerleaders to our roost, but you also may be aware that I won't be here to chastise you. Provided you are smart. There's pro-phylactics in the kitchen underneath the drawer with the can opener and the cheese thingy. Hang on, I'll show you. *(GLEN, 46, enters in a bathrobe.)* Okay-- *(He sees DEWEY's condition.)* Jesus Christ! *(He rushes over but pauses, afraid to touch DEWEY.)* Oh Jesus. Oh fuck. Jesus fuck. Fuck. Fuck, Dewey, what the fuck *happened!*

(DEWEY looks at GLEN, then at the helmet, then at GLEN.)

DEWEY. I don't know.

(With that, he passes out. GLEN half-catches him, straining under the weight. He struggles to get DEWEY to the sofa. Blackout.)

Scene 5

(Ruby's diner. Just before dawn. RICHIE, 44 and unshaven, sits alone at a booth. He is wearing a Dallas Cowboys cap, a plaid shirt and a taxi driver's ID tag. He stares ahead: lips set in a line. His hands grip a steaming coffee cup. They begin to constrict around the cup, as though he is trying to stretch his fingers. After a moment of this, his hands and arms begin to shake from the effort. Coffee slops over the side of the cup and across his hands, spilling onto the table. OPAL, a waitress, 27, approaches.)

OPAL. You... *(Her word dissolves into a yawn. She shakes her head.)* You doin all right? *(RICHIE does not acknowledge her. She looks down, sees the spilled coffee, and gasps.)* Oh my god your hands. *(She takes her towel and wipes the table and his hands. He remains impassive, except that she can't pry his hands off the cup.)* Let me see your hands. Mister. Let me see. *(She pries his fingers open. He does not otherwise move, still staring straight ahead. She examines his hands.)* You burned yourself. *(She looks at him.)* You burned your hands. *(Slowly, he looks down at his hands.)* Are you going to be all right?

(Small pause. He looks at her. Blackout.)

Scene 6

(A hospital. The ICU waiting room. Cheap faux-wood furniture. Magazines, a vase of flowers. GLEN and STEIN, 29, a resident.)

STEIN. We don't know.

GLEN. What does that mean?

STEIN. That's really all it means. We don't know. We might not know for--

GLEN. Well can you take a *guess?*

STEIN. It would be unfair of me, Mr. Provine, to give you information that wasn't one hundred percent truthful.

GLEN. When will you know?

STEIN. I--

GLEN. You don't know.

*(STEIN shakes his head. Small pause. GLEN nods, walks around the
room a moment, then picks up the vase and smashes it to the
ground. Silence.)*

STEIN. I'm sure--

GLEN. *Fuck you sure.*

(Small pause.)

STEIN. If you'd rather not talk to me...*(Small pause.)* There are
staff people designated to handle this situation. You can talk to them if
you want.

GLEN. Yeah?

STEIN. I'm not saying they're going to give you an answer that will
make you any happier, but they're better trained than I am.

GLEN. Yeah, cause you're pretty shitty at it.

STEIN. I know. I'm sorry for that. I was never very good at...this.
I got bad marks all the time for bedside manner. But I got good grades
for everything else. I got straight A's the rest of the time. It's just my
bedside manner that's...problematic. I'm sorry. Please try and see past
that. Please try and see what I'm saying objectively. I can assure you
that my...my...*demeanor*...has nothing to do with my ability to practice
medicine, or my, my qualifications, or the extremely competent manner
in which the hospital is going to take care of...of...*(He looks at his clipboard.)* Dewey.

(Small pause.)

GLEN. Any other helpful reminders written down there? Like, "Be nice"? Or, "Take dick out of pants before pissing"?

(Small pause.)

STEIN. Would you...*like* me to get someone?

(Small pause.)

GLEN. Get the fuck out of here.

STEIN. All right. *(Small pause.)* You can sit here, or...You can go home. You don't have to stay here. Some people like to stay, but others would prefer to go home, and I get the sense sometimes that people would rather go home, but they feel they can't. And I'm saying, that that's, it's not unhealthy. It's a normal emotion to feel, if my experience dealing with similar situations is worth anything. *(GLEN stares angrily at STEIN.)* All right.

(Small pause. STEIN exits.)

GLEN. Fucking asshole...

(He picks up one of the flowers, crumples it, and throws it on the floor. He sits, checks his watch, closes his eyes, and leans his head against the wall. Blackout.)

Scene 7

(The hotel room. Early morning. MIRANDA is alone in the bed. The phone rings. She picks it up.)

MIRANDA. Thank you. *(She hangs up and rolls over, searching sleepily for ROBERTA. When she realizes that ROBERTA is not there, she sits up.)* Shit...(She gets up, and goes to the bathroom door. From* *inside the bathroom, we hear a little scream. MIRANDA jumps back and closes the door, shouting:)* Sorry! *(She sits on the edge of the bed. After a moment, we hear a toilet flush. Then ROBERTA emerges from the bathroom, and, without looking at MIRANDA, starts putting on her clothes. Small pause.)* Sorry.

ROBERTA. That's okay.

(Small pause.)

MIRANDA. The door wasn't--

ROBERTA. I'm sorry.

MIRANDA. You don't have to be sorry, just that--

ROBERTA. I should've locked the door.

MIRANDA. Yes--I mean, no. But--

ROBERTA. It's okay.

MIRANDA. Okay. *(Small pause. ROBERTA still isn't looking at MIRANDA.)* How did you sleep?

ROBERTA. I didn't very much.

MIRANDA. Oh. I'm sorry.

ROBERTA. It's okay. It's not your fault.

MIRANDA. I didn't sleep very much, either.

ROBERTA. You were asleep. I saw you sleeping.

MIRANDA. Well, yeah, once we...decided to go to sleep, I fell asleep.

ROBERTA. I know.

MIRANDA. But that wasn't for very long.

ROBERTA. You must be tired.

MIRANDA. Yes. Not as tired as you, but--

ROBERTA. I'm not tired.

MIRANDA. You didn't sleep.

ROBERTA. I'm not tired.

(Small pause.)

MIRANDA. Your flight's not till one.

ROBERTA. I know.

MIRANDA. You've got plenty of time.

ROBERTA. I don't want to be late again.

MIRANDA. The airport's fifteen minutes away.

ROBERTA. I'm not taking any chances.

(Pause.)

MIRANDA. We could get breakfast.

ROBERTA. I'm not hungry.

MIRANDA. You'll get hungry.

ROBERTA. I have pie.

MIRANDA. We could eat somewhere. *(Small pause.)* We could go somewhere like a hotel.

ROBERTA. This is a hotel.

MIRANDA. A hotel where they serve breakfast. Like the Four Seasons.

ROBERTA. You go to places like that?

MIRANDA. Sometimes.

ROBERTA. I don't like them.

MIRANDA. I wouldn't turn down an offer for breakfast there if I got one.

ROBERTA. I'm not offering.

MIRANDA. I know. *I* am.

ROBERTA. I hate the Four Seasons.

MIRANDA. It's the nicest place I've ever eaten.

ROBERTA. How many times have you eaten there?

MIRANDA. What?

ROBERTA. You've eaten there a lot?

MIRANDA. Not a lot, I--

ROBERTA. People take you there.

MIRANDA. I've been taken there, sure.

(Small pause.)

ROBERTA. I ate at the Four Seasons in Los Angeles. There was a man in a suit having breakfast with a girl twenty years younger than him. She was wearing a leather miniskirt and lace stockings. I heard her ask him, "So where are you from?" He was from Cleveland. He was in town for business. He had never been to California before. He had a wife and two daughters. *(Small pause.)* He said they looked a little like her. *(Small pause.)* When they were done eating she gave him a business card and a kiss on the mouth. She was wearing knee-high boots, too. *(Small pause. MIRANDA bolts up, goes over to ROBERTA, and slaps her. Long pause.)* I'm sorry. *(Small pause.)* I'm very tired.

(Small pause.)

MIRANDA. I thought you weren't tired.
ROBERTA. Of course I'm tired.

(Small pause. ROBERTA looks at MIRANDA.)

MIRANDA. I'm going to give you breakfast. I don't want you to argue with me any more.
ROBERTA. Okay.
MIRANDA. Where do you want to go?
ROBERTA. Someplace close.
MIRANDA. We can go to my house. *(Small pause.)* We don't have to. We could...*(Small pause.)* We could stay here and finish the pie. I don't know how much is left...*(She looks at the pie on the nightstand. It is empty.)* Wow. We ate almost everything.
ROBERTA. Yes.
MIRANDA. We're going to have to go out. *(Small pause.)* You don't want to.
ROBERTA. I don't know.
MIRANDA. The pie's gone. I'm offering you the Four Seasons. My house is close by.
ROBERTA. I don't want to know where you live.

(Long pause. MIRANDA appraises ROBERTA.)

MIRANDA. Do your kids look like me?

ROBERTA. I don't have kids.

MIRANDA. Your husband? Does he look like me? *(ROBERTA looks at the floor.)* All right. *(Small pause.)* Don't tell him. Trust me on this. He won't understand. He might say it's sexy, he might even tell you he likes it, but really he'll want to rip your face off. *(ROBERTA is shaking her head.)* What.

ROBERTA. I'm divorced.

MIRANDA. Oh. *(Small pause.)* Then what the hell does it matter?

ROBERTA. It's not that.

MIRANDA. Then what is it.

(Small pause.)

ROBERTA. Will you come with me?

(Small pause.)

MIRANDA. Where?

(Blackout.)

Scene 8

(Bathroom at Ruby's. OPAL has a burn kit, and is treating RICHIE's hands.)

OPAL. Everyone thinks I'm crazy cause of the kit. I can't help it. It's like my thing to have it around. I always keep one with me. My brother in sixth grade saw his science teacher do an experiment where he put kerosene in a Sparklett's bottle, then dropped a match in and it shot like a flamethrower out of the top.Tommy said, "That's cool," and decided to try it at home with one of our Sparklett's bottles. But he wasn't paying good attention to the teacher's, you know, *measurements*, so he put in too much kerosene. Whoosh! He almos' burned his hand off. Second degree up and down his left hand, to the wrist. I told him that time, "Tommy, for a smart guy, you sure are dumb." He's smarter than me, but I never did anything *that* stupid... It's like we have the same total amount of stupid versus smart points, but my scale is a lot smaller than his. I might not do stuff that's, like, *really* smart, but I never do anything that's more than a *little* stupid. Tommy does really smart stuff, and to balance it out he does these total goofballs...*(Small pause. She looks at his hand.)* It's not too bad. You'll get better. *(She closes the kit up.)* Now I can tell them it came in handy, and they won't think I'm so dumb... You want something else to eat? Ruby said I can give you another cup of coffee. *(RICHIE shakes his head.)* Okay. Hey, you're a taxi driver? *(He nods.)* You must meet some interesting people.

(Small pause.)

RICHIE. Some.
OPAL. I bet. I meet some interesting people. Jeez I'm tired. I'm done soon. I've been on shift all night. I like the night shift better, though. You? *(He nods.)* How long you been on?
RICHIE. Since two.
OPAL. AM?
RICHIE. Nn.
OPAL. PM? Like, *yesterday? (He nods.)* Jeez Louise, you must be tired. *(She yawns.)* Yawning's supposed to be contagious. I don't believe it. You didn't yawn, did you?
RICHIE. No.
OPAL. But you must be tireder than me. How come you're not, like, falling asleep at the wheel? Lotta coffee. You sure you gonna make it home? You don't want another coffee? *(He shakes his head.)* Um, okay. I mean, okay. It's whatever you think is, uh, appropriate. *(Small pause.)* Your hand is gonna be okay.

(He nods. Small pause.)

RICHIE. Thanks.

OPAL. My pleasure. *(Small pause.)* You didn't move when it burned you. You just sat there like it was not burning you. You're not like...a *monk*, are you? One of the guys who feels no pain and can make his heart beat like five times a minute?

(Small pause.)

RICHIE. I'm not like that.

OPAL. Good. I mean, okay. Like, if you *were* a monk, that's okay, too. You don't meet too many monk taxi drivers.

RICHIE. I've never met any.

OPAL. Me neither. I've never met any taxi drivers.

RICHIE. Neither have I.

(Small pause. He smiles.)

OPAL. Oh. Oh! You're joking. Oh. *(She starts to laugh.)* That was really funny. I'm sorry, it *was* really funny, I'm just, sometimes, I'm tired, my reflexes aren't what they're supposed to be...

RICHIE. It's okay.

OPAL. You're the first taxi driver I ever talked to.

RICHIE. You're the first waitress--

OPAL. Oh come on, you must've talked to waitresses before. Everybody talks to waitresses. I got people askin me all the time personal stuff. It's ridiculous. I wanna say, "Hel*lo*, my phone number or my bra size is *not* on the menu, you can't ask for it special", but what can I do. You know what, though, I shouldn't worry about it. Those guys tip lousy anyway.

RICHIE. I wasn't going to say that.

OPAL. Oh. You weren't?

RICHIE. I was going to say, you're the first waitress who ever bandaged my hand.

OPAL. Oh. *(Small pause.)* Thank you.

RICHIE. Thank you.

OPAL. You're welcome. *(Small pause.)* You sure you don't want another coffee? Just to get rid of whatever sleep might creep up on you? You had a long night. Jeez Louise, two PM to five AM. That's a long shift. You must be wiped *out. (Small pause.)* Or... *(Small pause.)* Or I could get you some pie.

(Small pause. He smiles at her. She smiles back. Blackout.)

Scene 9

(The street corner. THE AMAZING TARQUIN. He flourishes a deck of cards.)

THE AMAZING TARQUIN. For my next trick, ladies and gentlemen--are you paying attention? I'm trying to build up your calf muscles, and in order to do so I need your cooperation. Everybody likes nice calves, especially Texans. *Moo!* And how, you ask in your tangy twangy drawl, do I purport to build the muscles in question? Why, by keeping you on your toes! *(He fans the cards.)* Pick a card! Got it? Good! *(He pockets the deck.)* Now note your card. You may as well tell me what it is. *(He frowns.)* The Queen of Spades. *(Small pause.)* I didn't expect that. *(He smiles.)* But nevertheless, the show must go on. It's all in the hands of Faith. And that's not so bad, have you ever seen Faith? What a looker. *(He takes the cards out of his pocket.)* The deck, ladies and gentleman, is utterly unstacked! It's honest, honest to God, or to your choice of higher or lower power, flower power for all I care. *(He fans the deck toward the audience so that we may see that faces of the cards. They appear normal.)* Now what we seek is the card you have chosen. You've got it in your pockets. Check and make sure I haven't prestidigitatorily purloined it. Check, go on, that's not checking. I know what you're doing with your hands in your pockets, you little rascals...

Good. Now, you know what your card is in the literal sense: the Black Queen. But I contend, labias and genitals, that it is far more. For what is it that we seek all the time? That's right, my fine and worthy Forth Worthians, we seek the answer. *(He conceals the cards.)* And when we seek, do we find? We do not. The card is gone from your pocket, friends, check and you'll see. Where is it now? Have I been searching in the wrong place? Mother, father, why have I forsaken myself, and for the sake of Pete, where's the card? *(He fans the deck toward us again: all the cards have gone blank.)* And the reply is, How the heck are we supposed to know?

(Blackout.)

Scene 10

(DEWEY's room at the hospital. DEWEY is unconscious. GLEN is sitting by his bedside.)

GLEN. They told me to talk quietly, so I've gotta keep it down. I don't know how talking to you is going to contribute to your your stress, but that's what they said. I always thought you were supposed to talk to people to wake them up. Like playing music for your plants. It seems to me now that it's probably a pile of horse droppings, like most things you see on television. *(Small pause.)* You learned more from television than anyone I ever knew. When you were five years old you walked into my room and said to me, "Dad, I learned two new words today." And I said, "What's that." And you said, "Cornucopia and bountiful." And then you said, "They both mean 'a lot.'"*(He smiles.)* You know something, Dewey, I didn't know what cornucopia meant until you told me. *(He laughs.)* They don't know shinola around here. I bet they could learn a lot from you. They don't know anything. All they know is to keep coming in and changing the bags. You're connected to everything in this place. *(GLEN touches a tube running from DEWEY's leg. He follows it with his eyes to a bag half-filled with urine, hanging at the edge of the bed. Amused.)* You watered the flowers. *(He looks at DEWEY.)* You're like a racehorse. *(Small pause.)* That's my boy. *(Small pause.)* When you were three your mom and I took you to visit Grandma Billie. We used to live next door to a cab driver. You don't remember that, you were too young. He was a fine guy, took us to the airport for half price. As soon as you-- *(He begins to laugh.)* As soon as you got in the cab, you just let it go, all over the cab, all over me, your mom's white pants, all over everything. Jiminy Cricket, we were so mad. The cab had cloth seats, soaked those up, too. We were ready to trade you in for a toaster, we were so mad. *(He laughs.)* We cleaned you up, and your mom shampooed out his back seat, and we went late to Grandma Billie's. And when you got there you threw up all over her couch. *(He laughs even harder.)* Oh Christ. We would've traded you in for a *broken* toaster. *(He laughs, crying at the same time; eventually, the crying takes over.)* Ohhhh *shit,* you goddamn, stupid, stupid, stupid, idiot, I told you to wear a *helmet.* You stupid idiot. You stupid idiot. I will be so happy to *beat* your disobedient ass, I am going to flay your fucking hide, you stupid, stupid, idiot, you stupid, stupid...*(He breaks off, crying. STEIN enters and stands in the doorway, watching him. After a moment, GLEN turns around and hurredly wipes his nose.)* Shit. What do you want...?

STEIN. I'm here to...would you like a tissue? *(He takes out a pocket-sized package of tissues.)* I carry them around when I'm on the ICU. A large number of people tend to cry in these situations.

GLEN. Is that right.

STEIN. Yes, it--

GLEN. I don't want a fucking tissue, I want to be alone with my son. I told you not to come in here.

STEIN . I'm aware of that, but Dr. Levenson wants to--

GLEN. Which one's that?

STEIN. The neurologist.

GLEN. The bald one?

STEIN. The...no. That's Dr. Sevitz, the plastic surgeon.

GLEN. I don't remember Levenson.

STEIN. He's...quite tall.

GLEN. Beer belly.

STEIN. He is somewhat...abdominous.

GLEN. Fat.

STEIN. He and I would like to run an MRI.

GLEN. Didn't you do that already?

STEIN. Not an MRI.

GLEN. What is it?

STEIN. Magnetic reso--it's a scan.

GLEN. Why?

STEIN. It's just to check if--

GLEN. I'm trying to find out, you know, what's being done to my son, because all I know is I sit here and assholes come in and out of here every hour to tell me to move out of the way so they can do something to him. I have a right to know what they're doing.

STEIN. Absolutely, you do.

GLEN. So what is it?

STEIN. It's to check the fluids in his tissues. Sometimes, internally, there can be bleeding, and we don't realize it at first, because it's slow and we're trying to gague what seems to be a more immediate trauma. In this case, the blow to the patient's head took precedence. But they're on their way up to move him to the MRI lab.

GLEN. *Now?*

STEIN. I would not describe the situation as urgent, per se, but there's no sense in wasting time if the patient--

GLEN. Don't call him the patient. He's not "the patient." His name is Dewey.

STEIN. Yes--

GLEN. You've got it written down on your clipboard, remember?

STEIN. I know, and--

GLEN. You sound like you're talking about...*somebody else.*

STEIN. I'm merely trying to--

GLEN. What's wrong with you? Don't you give a shit?

STEIN. I...there is a job here, Mr. Provine. I'm trying to do it. Please don't make it more difficult for me to help...

(Small pause.)

    GLEN. Dewey.

(Small pause.)

    STEIN. Yes.

(Pause. GLEN studies STEIN.)

    GLEN. Hey, do me a favor.

(Small pause.)

    STEIN. Mr. Provine?
    GLEN. Talk to me.

(Small pause.)

    STEIN. I am--
    GLEN. No, talk to me like Dewey.

(Small pause.)

    STEIN. Pardon?
    GLEN. You be Dewey. Go stand behind his head. When I ask him
questions, you answer for him.

(Small pause.)

    STEIN. I'm not sure I can do that.
    GLEN. There's a rule against it?
    STEIN. No, but--
    GLEN. Then do it.
    STEIN. Mr. Provine--

GLEN. Just--*do it.*
STEIN. While I would like to--
GLEN. Oh, fuck it. Forget it. Just forget about it.
STEIN. I'm sorry, I...
GLEN. Never mind.

(GLEN turns away. Pause. STEIN goes behind the headboard.)

STEIN. Okay. *(Small pause.)* Ask me something.

(Small pause.)

GLEN. Hey, Dewey.

(Small pause.)

STEIN. That wasn't a question.
GLEN. Yeah, but--just--I said *hi.*
STEIN. I know, I am trying to--
GLEN. Okay. Okay. Try again. *(Small pause.)* Go ahead.
STEIN. Go ahead what.
GLEN. *Hey,* Dewey.
STEIN. Hey. *(Small pause.)* Pop.
GLEN. "Dad".
STEIN. Dad.
GLEN. How you doing?
STEIN. Not...uh, not too well.
GLEN. No kidding. You look like shit.
STEIN. Dr. Sevitz expects that the lacerations to the--
GLEN. I didn't ask for a goddamn prognosis, I asked about--
STEIN. *(Overlapping with "I asked about...")* Okay. Okay. Okay.
(Small pause.) I feel like...like..."shit".
GLEN. I bet you do. When you were a kid and you hurt yourself, I used to tell you, "Squeeze my finger how much it hurts." And you'd squeeze it as hard as you could.

(Small pause.)

    STEIN. Okay.

(Small pause.)

    GLEN. Do you remember that?

(Small pause.)

    STEIN. Y--yes.
    GLEN. I miss that. I miss when you did that.

(Small pause.)

    STEIN. I...miss it, too?

(GLEN laughs.)

    GLEN. I dunno if Dewey'd say that.

(Small pause.)

    STEIN. What would he say.
    GLEN. He might say...he might say, Dad...Dad, I need thirty bucks.

(Small pause.)

    STEIN. Dad, I need--
    GLEN. *(Immediately)* No.
    STEIN. Okay.

(Small pause.)

    GLEN. What do you think of this stinkin hospital?

STEIN. Pardon--

GLEN. Don't say pardon, Dewey'd never say pardon, he'd say, *What?*

STEIN. This hospital is not--

GLEN. I'm just asking Dewey, what you think of--

STEIN. Well, *I* don't think it's a stinking--

GLEN. I'm not asking you, I'm asking--

STEIN. Mr. Provine, I don't think--

GLEN. You're not you. You're Dewey.

STEIN. Fine, and--I know--and, okay. Fine. Then, *Dad,* I think that, especially considering all that's going on here, how short-staffed they are, I think I've been treated very well here.

GLEN. Who thinks that.

STEIN. I do. Dewey. I'm Dewey.

GLEN. You sound pretty goddamn miserable.

STEIN. Of course I am! I've got a crack in my skull and broken ribs and a broken nose and I'm lying here all alone.

GLEN. All right...

STEIN. *And I don't know what to do about it,* all right? I don't know *what* to do!

GLEN. All right, all right--

STEIN. I mean, it may not be perfect, but everybody around me is trying--

GLEN. For *chrissake*--forget it. *Forget it. (Pause.)* What about this doctor you have?

(Small pause.)

STEIN. What about him?

GLEN. Between you and me, Dewey, I think he might need to get laid.

STEIN. I don't--

GLEN. Maybe he's married.

STEIN. He isn't.

GLEN. How do you know.

STEIN. He's not wearing a ring, is he?

GLEN. Some people don't wear rings.

STEIN. He would.

GLEN. Yeah? How do you know?

STEIN. He's that type of person.

GLEN. What do you know about him?

STEIN. I'm taking a guess!

GLEN. You know him pretty well, huh? Then tell me this: why doesn't he give a shit about *you!*

STEIN. He does, he--

GLEN. It sure doesn't show.

STEIN. Have a little compassion.

GLEN. *I* should have compassion on him? He doesn't have compassion for you or for me, and I should take it easy on *him?* What the hell for!

STEIN. He *does* have compa--

GLEN. Yeah, he's *real good.*

STEIN. He--he's trying.

GLEN. *He stinks.*

(Pause)

STEIN. He wants to like me. He wants to like the people he deals with, that would be a privilege for him, if he could only heal people worth healing. But sometimes they're terrible people. He has learned not to ruin his own life because of the ruin in other people's lives. He used to do what you want him to do, and he used to want to slash his wrists every Friday. He learned not to. He sleeps with his arms around a pillow. Someone used to be there but she got bored and depressed listening to how horrible he felt all the time, and when she went to Phoenix, he decided not to let it get to him. That might make him a bad person but he can still treat patients with delicacy and precision, and ultimately, *Dad*, that's what's important. He'd like it if you approved, but he's more concerned with keeping me alive.

(Pause)

GLEN. That's what he thinks?
STEIN. Yes.

(Pause)

GLEN. Well, Dewey, I trust your judgment here. Your opinion is what matters, not mine.
STEIN. Try and see it his way. *(Small pause.)* Dad.

(Small pause.)

GLEN. Yeah...*(Small pause. GLEN looks at STEIN.)* He's okay. He's a little weird, but he's all right.

(Small pause.)

STEIN. Thanks.
GLEN. Don't thank me. Thank him.
STEIN. Thank you, Doctor. *(Small pause.)* Uh. You're welcome.

(Small pause. They look at each other. Blackout.)

Scene 11

(The hotel room.)

MIRANDA. What are you going to tell them?
ROBERTA. I don't know.
MIRANDA. Because you can't walk in there and--
ROBERTA. Maybe I can.
MIRANDA. No. No. No.
ROBERTA. If I do--

MIRANDA. You didn't *do* anything.

ROBERTA. I did.

MIRANDA. But--no. No, you didn't.

ROBERTA. I--

MIRANDA. You weren't driving.

ROBERTA. No, but--

MIRANDA. You didn't have control over the car.

ROBERTA. I could have told him to stop.

MIRANDA. That's not up to you.

ROBERTA. I'm the passenger, he's the driver, he goes and stops when I tell him to.

MIRANDA. Not with things like this. This is not the normal, you know, *course of events.*

ROBERTA. I know...

MIRANDA. And, so, if you told him to--to--run the guy over on purpose, would he listen to you?

ROBERTA. Who.

MIRANDA. The driver.

ROBERTA. If I told him to run over a bicyclist?

MIRANDA. Yes.

ROBERTA. That's not what--

MIRANDA. I'm giving you an example. Okay? Are you paying attention? If, for example, you told him to run him over on purpose, he wouldn't. So you can see as well as I do that a taxi driver doesn't have to listen to everything you tell him.

ROBERTA. Okay, but--

MIRANDA. It's not within your control, you didn't do it--

ROBERTA. *(Overlapping with "do it")* It doesn't matter.

MIRANDA. It matters!

ROBERTA. It doesn't matter.

MIRANDA. You're acting like a goddamn idiot, so I would appreciate your attention here.

ROBERTA. Don't say that, you barely know me--

MIRANDA. I do know you. What did you tell me last night? *(Pause.)* Okay. And so don't tell me I don't know you.

ROBERTA. That was completely different.

MIRANDA. It wasn't. Now let's think for a minute. You need to leave.

ROBERTA. No...

MIRANDA. Hello! That's what you were doing before! You were going to get on a plane! Now you want to go to the police! While we're at it, you want to stop at a *church* along the way?

ROBERTA. I was going to get on a plane. I'm not getting on the plane any more.

MIRANDA. You have plenty of time. It's not even nine AM.

ROBERTA. I'm not going.

MIRANDA. You are.

(MIRANDA goes to the phone, dials.)

ROBERTA. What are you--

MIRANDA. I need a taxi to the airport.

ROBERTA. Stop--

(She goes to hang up but MIRANDA hangs it up first.)

MIRANDA. What am I doing, *I'll* drive you to the airport...

(MIRANDA finds one shoe, puts it on, starts looking for the other.)

ROBERTA. Listen, I'm not going.

MIRANDA. I'm not talking to you about this.

ROBERTA. I changed my mind. I'm allowed to do that.

MIRANDA. Where's my shoe...

ROBERTA. I wanted to get on the plane. I was *going* to get on the plane, but then I was late, and I--

MIRANDA. *(Muttering, overlapping with "and I".)* I *know* you were late, I took down your, your, your stupid...where the fuck is my *shoe*...

ROBERTA. No but listen. I came back here last night. I wanted to go to England. I thought I would flee the country. I've never even been to England.

MIRANDA. You'll like it, it's weird and depressing...

(MIRANDA goes into the bathroom.)

ROBERTA. Then I couldn't get on the plane. Because of you. You see? And then you came here, and I was scared of that, too. Then this morning I was scared again. Then you hit me, and now things are different.

(MIRANDA emerges with the shoe.)

MIRANDA. It was in the bathtub...

(She sits on the bed and puts it on.)

ROBERTA. You made all the difference.
MIRANDA. I did.
ROBERTA. Yes.
MIRANDA. Cause I hit you.
ROBERTA. I needed it.
MIRANDA. You're nuts, you know that? You're insane!
ROBERTA. I'm not going to go to England.
MIRANDA. You'll lose your job.
ROBERTA. I hate my job.
MIRANDA. You were crying in the airport yesterday.
ROBERTA. I was crying everywhere all the time.
MIRANDA. That's that's that's too bad.
ROBERTA. I'm not any more, though.
MIRANDA. Well *congratulations.*
ROBERTA. Please come with me.
MIRANDA. Why?
ROBERTA. I'm afraid to go alone.
MIRANDA. You should be. They're going to arrest you.

ROBERTA. We don't know what'll happen.

MIRANDA. Look, if you want to go turn yourself in for something you didn't do, I'm not going to be around when you do it.

ROBERTA. But you were the one who convinced me.

MIRANDA. What!

ROBERTA. You did, you--

MIRANDA. Hang on.

ROBERTA. You--

MIRANDA. Back up.

ROBERTA. I--

MIRANDA. Slow down.

ROBERTA. If it wasn't for last night, I'd be on the plane right now, escaping from this.

MIRANDA.	ROBERTA.
Which is exactly what you need to do.	Now I know that I can't just do that, you said--

MIRANDA. I'm telling you *now* to leave!

ROBERTA. There was a *kid* on a *bicycle.*

MIRANDA. I'm very sorry but so what!

ROBERTA. It was my car.

MIRANDA. It was a car that you were in.

ROBERTA. I could still go to jail.

MIRANDA. Ohhhhhh*god! You people!*

ROBERTA. What "people"?

MIRANDA. I *never* saw anything like this before I moved to Texas. I *swear,* I never saw *anything* like this before I moved to Texas! Are you a Jesus freak?

ROBERTA. I wouldn't have done did what I did last night if I was a Jesus freak.

MIRANDA.. Oh please. My first time was with a nun.

(Very small pause.)

ROBERTA. Really?

MIRANDA. Down here, if it's not one thing, it's another. It's like the South but the rules are all fucked up. It's "frontier morality". It's *bullshit,* you don't have to go to the *police.*

ROBERTA. It's not Jesus, or the frontier, or anything, it's just the right thing to do.

MIRANDA. Please! Please, lady. Stop having a psycho moment and thinking you're going to go to heaven if you do something that looks to you like good. It's not good. It's stupid. He's probably fine, he got a day off from work.

ROBERTA. He's a *kid.*

MIRANDA. Then he stayed home from school. It's not going to clear your conscience, because guess what, *you didn't do anything!* So get your head straight, and go to your business meeting, and when you relax, please call me when you get back, because I like you, I want you, I don't know what the hell I'm saying, but I want to see you, I'd like to see you a lot, and I'd like to have another night like last night. Listen to me. I want to see you. But in person. I won't visit you once a month in jail. So *will you please pack your bag.*

(Pause)

ROBERTA. Roberta. *(Pause)* That's my name.
MIRANDA. I know what it is, I reissued your ticket.
ROBERTA. You called me "lady".

(Small pause.)

MIRANDA. I know. *(Small pause.)* I'm sorry. *(Small pause.)* It's what I call customers when I'm angry at them. *(Small pause.)* You're not a customer. I forgot myself.

(Pause)

ROBERTA. What's your name?

(Small pause.)

MIRANDA. It was on my nametag.
ROBERTA. I forgot it. I was upset at the airport.

(Small pause.)

MIRANDA. Miranda.

(Small pause.)

ROBERTA. Miranda.

(Long pause.)

MIRANDA. Can you come here?

(After a pause, ROBERTA comes to MIRANDA and embraces her. MIRANA kisses ROBERTA's forehead and sits her on the bed.)

ROBERTA. The worst possible things could happen.
MIRANDA. In general? *(ROBERTA nods.)* Yes. But they don't usually.
ROBERTA. That's true in your experience.
MIRANDA. Yes.

(ROBERTA looks at MIRANDA..)

ROBERTA. You're much younger than me.
MIRANDA. Not that much.
ROBERTA. Yes. Much. *(Small pause.)* Why do you like me?
MIRANDA. I don't know.
ROBERTA. Do I remind you of someone?
MIRANDA. Not really.
ROBERTA. I thought maybe I reminded you of the nun.

(MIRANDA laughs.)

MIRANDA. She wasn't a habit-wearing nun, nun. She taught biology at my high school.

ROBERTA. Oh my god, your high school, that's appalling.

MIRANDA. Why?

ROBERTA. Because it's irresponsible.

MIRANDA. It was my idea.

ROBERTA. Still.

MIRANDA. She was very pretty, with low self-esteem.

ROBERTA. How do you know?

MIRANDA. I could tell. I can tell things like that.

ROBERTA. Do I have low self-esteem?

(MIRANDA smiles.)

MIRANDA. You *are* very pretty.

ROBERTA. That's not what I asked. *(MIRANDA kisses ROBERTA.)* You like me.

MIRANDA. What difference does it make?

ROBERTA. But you do.

MIRANDA. I do. *(Long pause.)* You could go to jail.

(Pause)

ROBERTA. I thought I didn't do anything wrong.

MIRANDA. I'm not a lawyer. I don't know anything about the law. *(Small pause.)* I don't know, but I don't want to ask them.

(Small pause.)

ROBERTA. I need to talk to someone.

MIRANDA. Talk to me. *(ROBERTA gently shakes her head. Small pause.)* You're a piece of work.

ROBERTA. Yes.

(They look at each other.)

MIRANDA. Okay. *(Small pause.)* Then who *can* you talk to?

(Small pause. ROBERTA goes to the phone, picks it up. Blackout.)

Scene 12

(OPAL's house. RICHIE is sitting at her kitchen table, eating a slice of pie.)

OPAL. I love their pie. Do you like it? *(RICHIE nods.)* All they had was peach. They didn't have the raspberry.

RICHIE. That's okay.

OPAL. The raspberry's good. It's the best. Miguel has this thing for raspberries, they're like his favorite ingredient. Ruby had to tell him quit puttin raspberries in everything, everything you make tastes like raspberries, you can't put raspberries in the burgers. So when he makes a raspberry pie you know it's going to be good.

(RICHIE finishes his pie.)

RICHIE. Thank you.

OPAL . You're welcome.

RICHIE. Thanks a lot.

OPAL. You're welcome again. You look pretty tired. You can lie down in the back if you want. *(He looks at her.)* You don't have to, though. If you want, I'm saying, there's a bed in the back, it's not my bedroom, but you can lie there for a little.

(Small pause.)

RICHIE. You live here by yourself.

OPAL. It used to be me and my brother. Now it's just me.

RICHIE. Tommy.

OPAL. What?

RICHIE. Your brother.

OPAL. Oh. Oh yeah. *(She smiles at him.)* Good memory. Yeah, Tommy. You want some more?

RICHIE. No thanks.

OPAL. Do you need to get home or something? Or do you want to lie down? There's a bed.

RICHIE. In the back.

OPAL. Yeah.

RICHIE. You like pie?

OPAL. Yeah.

RICHIE. Peach.

OPAL. Yeah. But not as much as the raspberry.

RICHIE. Peach is my favorite.

(Small pause.)

OPAL. It is?

RICHIE. Yeah.

OPAL. I thought raspberry was your favorite.

RICHIE. Why'd you think that?

OPAL. Cause you order it all the time.

(Small pause. RICHIE smiles at her.)

RICHIE. I do, huh?

(She smiles, blushes. Small pause.)

OPAL. There's some more in the kitchen.

RICHIE. You have some too?

(She smiles at him, gets up, and takes the plate in the kitchen.)

OPAL. (O.S.) Shows you what I know...here I am thinking your favorite is one and really it's the other.

RICHIE. You never have the peach.

OPAL. (O.S.) He rotates the flavors, there's always two and one's always raspberry cause it's Miguel. But he's on an eight day rotation. I remember them even though it's a pain to keep straight, always shifting one day up the week. Today we had peach. Tomorrow's chocolate. Then strawberry, banana cream, lemon meringue, cherry, apple, boysenberry. *(She appears through the door with a piece of peach pie and two forks.)* Then back to peach. At Thanksgiving you get pumpkin thrown in and Jeez Louise the whole schedule's shot to hell. *(She sits and they start to eat.)* If you're still hungry after this I can get you some more. Or there's stuff left over from yesterday I brought home. There's some chicken and a half a salad. It's good but you might not like it. It's got raspberries in it. *(They smile at each other.)* How's your hand.

RICHIE. It's okay, I think.

OPAL. That's good. I'm the burn specialist.

RICHIE. Yes you are.

OPAL. What you really need to heal yourself is rest. Everybody needs rest, but especially the infirm.

RICHIE. Maybe I'll lie down.

OPAL. In back there's a bed.

RICHIE. Yeah.

OPAL. It used to be Tommy's bed. Not anymore. Don't worry, I changed the sheets.

RICHIE. That's good to know.

OPAL. We were very *hygienic* kids. We learned it at home.

RICHIE. Yeah?

OPAL. Oh yeah. We learned it.

RICHIE. From...from your mom?

OPAL. Oh no. Not my mom. My mom's dead.

RICHIE. Sorry--

OPAL. That's okay. I never knew her, she died when I was born.

RICHIE. Oh...

OPAL. Yeah, it...yeah.

(Small pause.)

RICHIE. Your dad.

OPAL . My dad? Well, no. I mean...no. I mean, he couldn't. He's gone, you know? He couldn't.

(He looks at her.)

RICHIE. Okay.

OPAL. Yeah. He's gone. Mom's dead. Tommy's somewhere in Seattle. *(Small pause.)* It's a weird thing. She died, and then he *left,* and...me and Tommy lived with some other people. Uh, yeah. It was weird. My dad, he didn't do so good after my mom died, I mean...he was a lot older. She was like, twenty-five, and he was like thirty-eight, and... This is what Tommy said, but he was like *two* when it happened, so how's he know so much. I guess he knows from the, the *people* we lived with, the Powells. Tommy said--and, you know, I don't know why I listened, because he said crap all the time, like "dad's a millionaire." Kids say stuff like that when they're...hurt, or...whatever. But Tommy said that my dad just...*went off*...you know, like--*(She taps her head.)*--after my mom died. They put him somewhere, uhm, we never heard from him. I don't know what's wrong with him except Tommy said he talked a lot, and well, what's wrong with that, I mean, Jeez Louise, *I* talk a lot, too, and that's not... anything, it's just...friendly. *(Pause)* How bout you, you got a family?

RICHIE. Two kids.

(She looks at him.)

OPAL. Oh yeah?
RICHIE. Mm-hm.

(Small pause.)

OPAL. So, uh--your--your *wife--(He shakes his head.)* Oh, yeah.

Okay. Just--you know. I mean, it's--you can still have a nap. As long as--but, I mean--it's okay. It's okay.

(Small pause.)

    RICHIE. She lives in Amarillo.

    OPAL. Divorced. *(He nods. She sighs with relief.)* Oh thank god. *(He looks at her.)* I mean--I'm--I mean--*(He starts to laugh. She laughs, too, embarrassed at first but eventually giving in.)* Oh man. Oh, man. Oh, jeez...I'm...I'm--

    RICHIE. It's okay.

    OPAL. Cause...you never know. You meet these...*types.*

    RICHIE. What types.

    OPAL. You know, in the restaurant.

    RICHIE. Like me?

    OPAL. No, not like you. Nobody like you. But you can't tell. I had a feeling about you, but, you know, who am I, a prophet? I could be wrong. You don't look like the *type,* but...you know...*(Small pause.)* It's Dallas, everybody's in a way here.

(Small pause.)

    RICHIE. You had a feeling about me. *(Pause. RICHIE's beeper goes off. He looks at it.)* Can I use your phone?

    OPAL. Sure. *(She points to the kitchen. He goes. She looks after him, then at the plate. She chews her lip nervously. She jabs the remains of the pie with her fork. RICHIE is talking softly offstage. She looks back in the kitchen. She takes the fork and scarfs down the rest of the pie, holding the plate up to her mouth and scraping the last crumbs in. She wipes her mouth, adjusts her hair, wipes the corners of her mouth again. She looks at the kitchen, hears him coming, turns around non-chalantly as though she has been ignoring him. He emerges looking shocked and dazed, and stands in the doorway. She turns to face him. Small pause.)* Everything all right? *(Small pause.)* Are you okay?

    RICHIE. I have to talk to someone.

(Small pause.)

　　OPAL. You can talk to me.

(He looks at her.)

　　RICHIE. No. Not you. There's a lady I have to talk to.
　　OPAL. A lady?
　　RICHIE. I don't know how she found me. *(Small pause.)* They called me from the dispatcher's and connected me. *(Small pause.)* A lady I drove last night wants to talk to me.

(Small pause.)

　　OPAL. Why? *(Small pause.)* Did she leave something in the cab? *(He shakes his head.)* Then what does she want from you?
　　RICHIE. She wants to meet me.
　　OPAL. What?
　　RICHIE. She's at the Four Seasons.

(Small pause.)

　　OPAL. That's very strange.

(Small pause.)

　　RICHIE. Yeah. It is.

(Small pause.)

　　OPAL. Did she stiff you?
　　RICHIE. No.
　　OPAL. She didn't give you a tip...
　　RICHIE. She gave me a big tip.
　　OPAL. So what then?

(Pause)

    RICHIE . I'm going to meet her.

(Small pause.)

    OPAL. You are?

(Pause. He looks at her.)

    RICHIE. Will you come with me?

(Small pause. Blackout.)

Scene 13

(The hospital. DEWEY's room. The bed is empty, and GLEN is alone, dozing. Enter STEIN. He watches GLEN for a moment, and is about to leave when GLEN stirs and rubs his eyes.)

    GLEN. ...okay, I'm awake, okay...
    STEIN. I had no intention of--
    GLEN. Where's Dewey?
    STEIN. He's not back yet.
    GLEN. Why not?
    STEIN. Mr. Provine, I came to tell you--

(GLEN stands up.)

    GLEN. What's going on. What's with Dewey?
    STEIN. There's some new--
    GLEN. Is he alive?
    STEIN. What?

GLEN. IS HE OKAY.

STEIN. Yes! Yes. He's alive.

GLEN. Then why didn't you say that!

STEIN. I--I'm sorry. He's alive.

GLEN. Jesus...

STEIN. That's not it. He's alive. There have been some new developments, and--

GLEN. What does that mean?

STEIN. Just that some new...details...have arisen.

GLEN. "Details"?

STEIN. Yes, and--

GLEN. Will you stop pussyfooting and--

STEIN. I'm sorry, I--okay, I'll just say it--

GLEN. Say it!

STEIN. Okay! *(Small pause.)* Dewey has a bone tumor. *(Long pause.)* Did--uh--did you hear me?

GLEN. *(Simultaneous with "hear me".)* Yes. *(Small pause.)* What?

STEIN. He has a Ewing's sarcoma.

GLEN. What the fuck is that.

STEIN. It's a type of bone cancer.

(Pause)

GLEN. Why does he have *that.*

(Small pause.)

STEIN. I really...don't know.

(Pause)

GLEN. He's seventeen.

(Small pause.)

STEIN. Yes.

GLEN. And you're telling me he has *cancer?*

STEIN. This is a certain type of cancer that appears most in adolescents.

GLEN. It's common?

STEIN. Not exactly.

(Small pause.)

GLEN. Is he going to die?

STEIN. If it's caught early enough, the survival rate is good. Two-thirds of cases go on to become long-term--

GLEN. *Two-thirds?* You want me to be *happy* about that? *(Pause)* What if it isn't caught early enough?

STEIN. It depends.

GLEN. Depends on what.

STEIN. On how far it has spread.

GLEN. How far has it spread.

STEIN. We don't know yet.

GLEN. When will you know!

STEIN. Soon.

GLEN. *When! (Pause. STEIN looks at the floor.)* Shit...

(Small pause.)

STEIN. We weren't sure before. When Dewey arrived we took a series of x-rays. I noticed what looked like a tumor, but I wasn't sure. *(Small pause.)* I was trying to deal with a lot at once. At the time of admission I was not looking for cancer.

GLEN. No shit. *(Small pause. Quietly.)* What the *fuck. (Small pause.)* It's in his bones.

STEIN. His femur. His leg.

GLEN. Which leg.

STEIN. The left.

GLEN. Just the one?

STEIN. Yes.

GLEN. Well that's good. He's a righty. Just the left, okay. He can... *(Small pause. GLEN begins to laugh.)* He can hop. He'll have one leg. Oh, sure... Hop! Hop!

(GLEN laughs harder. STEIN watches him.)

STEIN. Are you...okay? *(GLEN laughs even harder.)* All right, well, if you are...*(Small pause. GLEN is laughing.)* At some point, when you're ready, we should...uh...there are some things we should...we should talk about.

GLEN. *(Laughing)* Yeah...

(Small pause. GLEN continues to laugh.)

STEIN. Should we...talk about them later?

GLEN. *(Laughing) Cancer?*

(Small pause.)

STEIN. Uh. Yes.

(GLEN is still laughing. As he brings himself under control:)

GLEN. And you only know about this cause he got *hit by a car.*

(Small pause.)

STEIN. ...yes. I suppose that's true.

(They look at each other. Blackout.)

END OF ACT I

Act II

Scene 1

(The AMAZING TARQUIN. He holds a top hat.)

THE AMAZING TARQUIN. And thus we begin again to spin again, Finnegan. But things have *changed,* haven't they? And speaking of change: *(From thin air, he plucks a coin, which he deposits in the top hat.)* I am wealthy, dugongs and manatees, independently wealthy, which is why your contribution is not charity but a recognition of the great art that your retinas retain. *(Another coin, into the hat.)* My grandfather, I'll have you know, was an oil magnate. He attracted oil. Texas is the most oleaginous state in the union, friends, and if you don't believe me then have a local taco. *(Another coin, into the hat.)* Grandpa was greasy, uncle was unctuous, father was fatty. I was destined from the very beginning, the first born son of a first born son of a first born son...and *so on!* I was the adipose-ter child for the family name! *(Another coin, into the hat.)* But there are some members of the clan-- *(He smiles.)*--so I've heard--who haven't a penny in their poor names. *(Another coin, into the hat.)* It's a lesson to be learned, Hades and Genuflect: that nice things are fleeting. *(Another coin, into the hat.)* Fleet like deer. Fleet like the Navy. Fleet like the largest financial corporation in the Commonwealth of Massachusetts, which, incidentally, handles my affairs--not because one man can't handle multiple affairs--

if he were alive Jack Kennedy would vouch for that--but because I'd rather die than give my money to the State of Texas. *(Another coin, into the hat.)* "Alack," cry you, "not very patriotic!" But you forget, babies and bauble-tongues, in the manner of so many Texans, you forget: the Lone Star State is not a sovereign nation. *(Another coin, into the hat.)* Oh yes: I mess with Texas. *(Another coin, into the hat.)* I hope that you've gleaned the lesson from my familiar, familial tale. If not, I reiterate, once again, superfluously: hold on to your money, because it can disappear.

(With a smile, he turns the hat upside down. Nothing falls out. Blackout.)

Scene 2

(The restaurant of the Four Seasons Hotel. MIRANDA and ROBERTA are sitting and waiting.)

MIRANDA. You have to have some sort of plan.

ROBERTA. I know...

MIRANDA. What are you going to tell him?

ROBERTA. I can't write it out to begin with. First I have to see what his attitude is like--

MIRANDA. And then?

ROBERTA. And then we can negotiate from there.

MIRANDA. He might have a terrible attitude.

ROBERTA. Maybe.

MIRANDA. He might be a terrible person.

ROBERTA. He agreed to show up.

MIRANDA. He might not.

(Small pause.)

ROBERTA. You're edgier than I am. *(Small pause.)* It's not on your head, you know. It's not my choice, but you don't have to make this decision.

MIRANDA. You made a decision to come.

ROBERTA. I know.

MIRANDA. I told you not to.

ROBERTA. I made a decision--

MIRANDA. Yes.

ROBERTA. --but it wasn't *really* a decision.

MIRANDA. What do you mean, sure it was.

ROBERTA. Not *really.*

MIRANDA. Until this morning you had plans to flee the country.

ROBERTA. Just cause nobody put a gun to my head--

MIRANDA.	ROBERTA.
Not yet.	--doesn't mean I had the actual option. I'm a certain kind of person, I'm going to do certain things. You go home for Christmas. You might have the literal choice to go to Las Vegas instead, but you don't really.

MIRANDA. I *don't* go home for Christmas.

ROBERTA. That's the kind of person you are.

MIRANDA. *What* kind of person!

ROBERTA. The kind that doesn't go home for Christmas.

MIRANDA. And what kind of person are *you?*

ROBERTA. The kind that doesn't feel good about running over a kid. *(Small pause.)* You can go.

MIRANDA. I know.

ROBERTA. It has nothing to do with you, it's not your "character" I'm talking about. You're not at stake, it's me.

MIRANDA. I know it's you. I *know. (Small pause.)* That's *why* I'm edgier than you are.

(Small pause as they look at each other. OPAL and RICHIE enter, look-ing lost. ROBERTA spies them and stands up. RICHIE nods at her.

*He and OPAL go to the table. MIRANDA stands up to greet them.
There is a brief silence as they all look at each other. Suddenly
OPAL sticks her hand out.)*
OPAL. Well, hi. I'm Opal.

(Small pause. MIRANDA shakes OPAL's hand.)

MIRANDA. Miranda.
OPAL. Are we going to do introductions, or are we going to sit
down, or what.

(Small pause. ROBERTA and RICHIE are looking at each other.)

MIRANDA. Maybe...maybe we should have some breakfast.
OPAL. That sounds great. *(They all sit down: ROBERTA and
RICHIE at the center, OPAL flanking RICHIE, and MIRANDA flanking
ROBERTA.)* Although I'm not really hungry.
MIRANDA. Neither am I.
OPAL. Is anyone here hungry? *(She looks at RICHIE, who is still
looking at ROBERTA. To RICHIE.)* Are you hungry?
RICHIE. *(Distracted)* Huh...? *(He looks at the menu.)* I could eat
something.
OPAL. *(To ROBERTA.)* Not a big eater?
ROBERTA. Pardon?
OPAL. You look thin.
ROBERTA. Uh, no. I'm not...Okay. *(Small pause.)* Thanks.
OPAL. No problem.
MIRANDA. Is there a waiter here?
OPAL. He's probably busy.
MIRANDA. It's almost empty.
OPAL. You know, busy with a lot of things.

ROBERTA.	OPAL.
(To RICHIE.) Thanks for coming.	*(To MIRANDA.)* He's probably overworked.

(RICHIE nods at ROBERTA, then looks at MIRANDA as if to say, "What is she doing here?")

MIRANDA. I don't doubt it.

(ROBERTA glances at OPAL. RICHIE shrugs. As this is happening:)

OPAL. Waiters get stuck with a lot of jobs that they're not supposed to have, but they do them anyway.

MIRANDA. I know. I was a waitress.

OPAL. Yeah?

MIRANDA.	ROBERTA.
(To OPAL.) In high school.	*(To RICHIE.)* Maybe we should--

OPAL. Oh.

RICHIE. No, I--*(Everyone looks at him. Small pause.)* Uh. I could eat.

(A WAITER approaches. He is played by the same actor who plays DEWEY. RICHIE stares at him.)

WAITER. Good morning, everyone.

OPAL. Hi.

WAITER. Can I start you off with something to drink?

MIRANDA. I'll have a bloody Mary.

OPAL. Diet Coke, please.

WAITER. Oooookay...*(To ROBERTA.)* Ma'am?

ROBERTA. Water, pl--*(She looks up at the WAITER and falters. Softly.)* Please.

OPAL. *(To RICHIE.)* You want something? *(Slowly, RICHIE shakes his head. To the WAITER.)* That'll do us fine.

WAITER. I'll be back in a minute with your drinks.

OPAL. Thank you. *(The WAITER leaves.)* Seems like a nice guy. *(Silence)* I mean, who knows what he's really like. But he seems like a nice guy.

(Silence.)

MIRANDA. Yes.
OPAL. *(To RICHIE.)* You're not thirsty?
MIRANDA. Maybe we should--*(To ROBERTA.)* Would you like us to leave you two alone?
OPAL. *(To MIRANDA.)* Leave who?
MIRANDA. *(To ROBERTA.)* We can come back in a little bit.
ROBERTA. Maybe...
OPAL. *(To MIRANDA.)* Who's coming back.
MIRANDA. *(To OPAL.)* We can. You and me.
ROBERTA. *(To RICHIE.)* Is that okay?
OPAL. Why would we do that?
MIRANDA. If they want to be alone.
OPAL. Why would they want that?

(Small pause.)

RICHIE. *(To OPAL.)* Could I have a minute with her, maybe?

(Small pause. OPAL looks at ROBERTA, then at RICHIE.)

OPAL. You said you wanted to have a quick talk with her.
RICHIE. I do.
OPAL. What...I...

(Small pause.)

RICHIE. It won't take long.
OPAL. You said it was nothing important.
RICHIE. It's not a big deal.

(OPAL looks at ROBERTA.)

OPAL. Is it a big deal? *(ROBERTA looks at RICHIE.)* It's a big deal.

(To RICHIE.) Why didn't you tell me it was a big deal?

MIRANDA. We don't know if it's a big deal or not.
ROBERTA. *(Overlapping with "deal or not".)* Miranda.
MIRANDA. *(To ROBERTA.)* We don't.

OPAL.	ROBERTA.
Everybody here knows what's going on except me?	*(To MIRANDA.)* Don't--*(To OPAL.)* Look, we just need to talk for a minute.

RICHIE. Just give us a minute, Opal.

(Small pause.)

OPAL. I suddenly don't feel like I know anything about this.
MIRANDA. None of us do.
OPAL. But me especially.
ROBERTA. None of us know. Anything.

(Small pause. The WAITER returns with their drinks, which he hands out.)

WAITER. Okay...and, are we ready?
OPAL. We're not eating.
WAITER. Pardon? *(OPAL gets up and walks away. ROBERTA and MIRANDA look at RICHIE. ROBERTA looks at MIRANDA, who gets up and follows OPAL off.)* I'm sorry, is everything okay?
ROBERTA. We're not ready to order yet.
WAITER. Well, take your time, and I'll be back in a minute.

(He leaves. A moment of silence as ROBERTA and RICHIE stare at the table.)

ROBERTA. Thanks for coming down here. *(Small pause.)* I know I didn't give you a lot of choice, but...*(Small pause.)* Thanks for coming down.

(He looks at her.)

RICHIE. No. You didn't.

(Small pause.)

ROBERTA. Is that your girlfriend?
RICHIE. Not exactly.
ROBERTA. Your...?
RICHIE. We just met.
ROBERTA. Oh. *(Small pause.)* The woman I'm with...? I just met her, also. Last night.

(Small pause.)

RICHIE. That's funny.

(Small pause. ROBERTA reflects for a moment.)

ROBERTA. Yeah. It is a little strange.

(Lights crossfade to OPAL, sitting in the hotel lobby, clutching her bag. MIRANDA approaches and sits next to her.)

MIRANDA. You look pretty upset.
OPAL. Well, it *is* a pretty upsetting thing, here I am, and all of a sudden, it's "can you go wait outside", and *I* don't know what's going on, I mean Jeez Louise, if I wasn't supposed to be here then what did he invite me for?
MIRANDA. We didn't know he was going to show up with another person.
OPAL. Who? Who didn't know?
MIRANDA. Roberta.
OPAL. I didn't even know we were going to have *breakfast.* Richie said he needed to talk to this woman. I didn't know anything about *two*

women, and--*(Sudden beat.)* Is that his wife?

    MIRANDA. No.

    OPAL. Are *you* his wife?

    MIRANDA. No, I--

    OPAL. Because he *told* me he wasn't married. He said his wife lives in Amarillo, but people can say anything they want, and most of the time they can get away with it, especially if the other person involved is...is...I don't know...*blinded* by...I just assumed he was telling me the truth, but I guess I should know better than that by now. *(Small pause.)* Who *are* you?

    MIRANDA. I'm Miranda.

    OPAL. I know that, you *told* me that.

    MIRANDA. Are you--you're his--?

    OPAL. He's a customer.

(Small pause.)

    MIRANDA. Oh.

(Small pause.)

    OPAL. So what is...*this.*

    MIRANDA. She's...*(Small pause. Carefully.)* She was a...customer.

    OPAL. Of his?

    MIRANDA. ...yes.

    OPAL. She's a friend of yours.

    MIRANDA. ...yes.

    OPAL. He said he drove some lady to the airport last night.

    MIRANDA. That was Roberta.

    OPAL. So why are you here.

    MIRANDA. Moral support?

    OPAL. Moral support.

    MIRANDA. I think so.

(Small pause. OPAL looks at MIRANDA.)

OPAL. Is that what I'm here for?

(Crossfade back to ROBERTA and RICHIE.)

ROBERTA. But--
RICHIE. I don't think it's something you should get involved in.
ROBERTA. But I have a responsibility...
RICHIE. You don't.
ROBERTA. If you don't, then it's up to me to make sure that--
RICHIE. No.
ROBERTA. What if he dies? Have you thought about that?
RICHIE. Of course I thought about it.
ROBERTA. And?
RICHIE. And I don't know.
ROBERTA. Don't you think you should find out?
RICHIE. I don't know his name, I didn't get a good look at him--
ROBERTA. I did.
RICHIE. He could be a million kids, in a million hospitals. This is a big city.
ROBERTA. We'll call them up.
RICHIE. Not "we".
ROBERTA. If you don't I will.
RICHIE. There you go again.
ROBERTA. Well I'm sorry, but you're not being--
RICHIE. Listen, I don't need this. I can leave here.

(The WAITER approaches.)

WAITER. Are we ready?
ROBERTA. *(To RICHIE.)* Please go ahead.
RICHIE. I don't want anything.
ROBERTA. We have to--*(To the WAITER.)* I'll have some wheat toast.
WAITER. Is that all?
ROBERTA. *(To RICHIE.)* Please eat something.

RICHIE. I'm not in the mood.

ROBERTA. I'm paying.

RICHIE. *(To WAITER.)* What's special?

WAITER. We have a breakfast special. It's a peach dumpling, sort of like a little pie--

(RICHIE puts his head in his hands.)

RICHIE. No, please, I don't want that.

WAITER. Okay. Well, we have--

RICHIE. Toast.

WAITER. White, wheat, sourdough--

RICHIE. *(Head in hands.)* Wheat.

WAITER. Two orders of wheat toast...

(He looks at them, indicating the empty seats.)

ROBERTA. They won't be joining us.

WAITER. Sure thing.

(Small pause. The WAITER doesn't move.)

ROBERTA. Yes?

WAITER. I'm very sorry, ma'am, we prefer if you order at least one entree per person. It's at the bottom of the menu.

ROBERTA. It is...? *(She looks at the menu.)* It is. Okay. Then I'll have...mmm...

RICHIE. *(Head in hands.)* Western omlette.

WAITER

Very good, sir... Ma'am? The peach dumpling's excellent.

ROBERTA. *(Overlapping with "excellent".)* No, please...just: how about: can I have the fruit plate? It's mixed fruit?

WAITER. Certainly. With cottage cheese?

ROBERTA. That's great. Thank you.

WAITER. You're very welcome.

(He takes the menus from them and exits. RICHIE still has his head in his hands.)

RICHIE. *(Quietly)* Fuck...*(He looks up at her.)* I can't stop thinking, everywhere I go I see...

(Small pause.)

ROBERTA. What.

RICHIE. Nothing. Nothing.

ROBERTA. It's going through my head, too.

RICHIE. Yeah...

ROBERTA. That's why we have to speak to someone. It's not going to leave you alone.

RICHIE. Sure it will.

ROBERTA. What are you going to tell your girlfriend?

RICHIE. She's not my girlfriend.

ROBERTA. But what are you going to--

RICHIE. She doesn't even know what's going on.

ROBERTA. Listen. Listen. What are you going to *tell* her?

RICHIE. Nothing.

ROBERTA. You can't not tell her. You can't lie to her.

RICHIE. I just *met* her!

ROBERTA. That's not a very good way to start off the relationship.

RICHIE. It's not a relationship!

ROBERTA. I'm just saying--

RICHIE. You don't get it... You can't walk into the hospital, give him a peck on the cheek and expect everything'll be fine. Forget it. I'll go to prison. *You* might go to prison, also. And believe me, you don't want to go there.

ROBERTA. If I *committed* something--

RICHIE. No. No. You *don't* want to go.

ROBERTA. You don't know what I want.

RICHIE. *Trust* me, you don't want that.

ROBERTA. You don't know what'll happen to us either, anything could--

RICHIE. Trust me on this. *(Small pause.)* Just trust me.

(Small pause. She looks at him quizzically.)

ROBERTA. You were in...*(He nods.)* Oh. *(Small pause.)* That's why you didn't want to stop the cab. *(He nods.)* Uh huh.

(Pause)

RICHIE. Do you see what I'm talking about now?

(Small pause.)

ROBERTA. Yes. *(Small pause.)* What did you do?
RICHIE. It's not...this is nothing like that. That's a totally *separate* thing. But that's not something anyone's going to understand. All they will see is, three years Huntsville. This is *Texas. (Small pause.)* Now, do you get it?
ROBERTA. Yes.
RICHIE. And I *swear* I didn't see him. He just *appeared.* I didn't even know anything had happened at first. You saw what happened, you were there.

(Small pause.)

ROBERTA. Yes. *(Small pause.)* I was there.

(Crossfade back to OPAL and MIRANDA. Long silence.)

MIRANDA. You didn't know?
OPAL. No. *(Pause)* He didn't tell me.

(Small pause.)

MIRANDA. Then I'm sorry I told you.

OPAL. No, it's good you did. *(Small pause. OPAL looks at MIRANDA.)* I just met him.

MIRANDA. When?

OPAL. This morning.

MIRANDA. People can surprise you.

OPAL. They sure can. Sure as heck. *(OPAL stands up.)* I think I'm going home.

MIRANDA. Are you sure?

OPAL. Yes.

MIRANDA. Did you drive here?

OPAL. I'll take a cab. *(She laughs.)* He drove me here in his cab. So I'm going home the same way. Except now I have to pay. *(She laughs again.)* God, this is so...*unnhhhh! (Small pause.)* I feel really stupid.

MIRANDA. It's not your fault.

OPAL. It's my fault for being this stupid. *(Small pause.)* What are they going to do?

MIRANDA. I don't know. Roberta wants to go to the police.

OPAL. Of course they should go to the police.

MIRANDA. That's what *she* says.

OPAL. Of course!

MIRANDA. It's not of course. I didn't want to come here to begin with.

OPAL. Why!

MIRANDA. First of all, it's not Roberta's fault. Secondly--

OPAL. Wait. You think it's his fault?

MIRANDA. He was driving.

OPAL. *She* didn't do anything about it!

MIRANDA. *He* was driving the car.

OPAL. But...*(She puts her hand on her forehead, walks around.)* I don't like this.

MIRANDA. I'm not...parceling out blame.

OPAL. You are!

MIRANDA. No, I'm saying that she didn't have to be the one to volunteer.

OPAL. I don't like this, at all.

MIRANDA. Nobody does.

OPAL. This isn't what I wanted. I don't know what I'm doing here. There was *pie,* and he *liked* it, and...*(She looks at MIRANDA.)* Tell them good luck.

(OPAL exits. MIRANDA starts after her, then stops. Crossfade back to RICHIE and ROBERTA. The WAITER is handing them plates. RICHIE has his head in his hands.)

WAITER. ..and the Western Omelette, careful, hot plate...
ROBERTA. Thank you. This looks good.
WAITER. Anything else--
RICHIE. *(Head still down.)* No thank you.
WAITER. Okay then. Enjoy.

(The WAITER exits.)

ROBERTA. He's gone.
RICHIE. *(Head still down.)* I know.

(He looks up.)

ROBERTA. I understand completely your position.
RICHIE. It--
ROBERTA. Hang on. Let me say something one second. *(Small pause.)* I understand where you're coming from. You have a peculiar set of circumstances. Okay. You can't go to the police, okay. I see why you're telling me this.

(Small pause.)

RICHIE. Then can we--
ROBERTA. One second. *(Small pause.)* All of this, everything you told me, makes sense. For you.
RICHIE. For you, too.

ROBERTA. No. For me, I need to talk to him. I need to see that he's okay.

RICHIE. Maybe he's not okay.

ROBERTA. Maybe not. Then I need to see *that,* too.

RICHIE. It's not going to make you feel better.

ROBERTA. I think it will.

RICHIE. Then what the hell am I supposed to do?

ROBERTA. We have a difference of opinion on this--

RICHIE. Yeah...

ROBERTA. That doesn't mean I'm going to sell you down the river.

RICHIE. Thanks a whole lot.

ROBERTA. I'm telling you the truth.

RICHIE. When you called me up you said you were going to call the cops immediately unless I met you.

ROBERTA. You tried to hang up on me.

RICHIE. I don't want any part of this!

ROBERTA. Don't--look--you don't have to get--

RICHIE. No, no, *yeah,* I do. I *do.* Because you're not my parole officer, or my mother--

ROBERTA. I know.

RICHIE. Then why are you *doing* this?

ROBERTA. I'm not doing anything, I'm just telling you that--

RICHIE. That you're going to go to the cops no matter what I say.

ROBERTA. For *me.* I'm going to the cops *for me.*

RICHIE. Oh, right, okay, you're going to tell them *you* were driving the cab.

ROBERTA. I'll tell them a friend drove me.

RICHIE. Who? Who drove you?

ROBERTA. A friend.

RICHIE. Like this *friend* you invent isn't going to be in a shitload of trouble?

ROBERTA. I'll say I was driving.

RICHIE. And what.

ROBERTA. And--all right, fine--and after I got to the airport, the friend took my car back.

RICHIE. And you hit the guy *when.*

ROBERTA. On the way to the airport.

RICHIE. And the friend was in the car *then,* right? *(Small pause.)* Right?

ROBERTA. Right.

RICHIE. So then: again: who is this friend? "We want to talk to this friend, ma'am. Would you mind giving us her name?"

(Pause)

ROBERTA. *(Quietly)* I'll figure something out.

RICHIE. No. No. You do not "figure it out." I was driving a *cab.* You don't think *somebody* saw? What if the guy saw? You tell them you were driving your car, you *lie* to the police, and you think, you *really think,* that they are not going to figure it out? You can't make it up. You're going to get caught. And I promise, no matter how *considerate* you are of my *situation,* that they're going to be knocking on my door within five hours of you arriving at the station. *(Small pause.)* And then what? *(Small pause.)* Huh?

(Pause)

ROBERTA. I can't let this go.

RICHIE. *Let* it go.

ROBERTA. I can't.

RICHIE. *Try.*

(Small pause.)

ROBERTA. I...I just can't.

(RICHIE stares at her. MIRANDA returns.)

MIRANDA. Can I sit down?

RICHIE. Where's Opal?

MIRANDA. *(To ROBERTA.)* Are you okay?

RICHIE. *(Overlapping with "okay".)* Where'd Opal go?
ROBERTA. *(To MIRANDA.)* Yes...
RICHIE. Lady.

(MIRANDA looks at RICHIE.)

MIRANDA. What?
RICHIE. Opal. Where is she.
MIRANDA. She left.
RICHIE . What?
MIRANDA. She wanted to go home.
RICHIE. Why'd she do *that?*
MIRANDA. She was very upset and she wanted to go home.
RICHIE. What?
MIRANDA. *(To ROBERTA.)* Are you all right?
ROBERTA. Yes...
RICHIE. *(To MIRANDA.)* Why was she upset?
MIRANDA. She was upset when she found out what was going on.

ROBERTA.   RICHIE.
(To MIRANDA.) I'm...I need to   Wait--*what?*
figure this out...

         MIRANDA.   RICHIE.
Let's go back to my place.   *(To MIRANDA.)* Lady. Lady.

MIRANDA. *(To RICHIE.)* My name is Miranda.
RICHIE. You *told* her what happened?
MIRANDA. Yes.
RICHIE. Oh, my holy fuck...
MIRANDA. *(To ROBERTA.)* We can go--
RICHIE. *Why'd* you do that?
MIRANDA. *(To RICHIE.)* She didn't know.
RICHIE. Yeah, I *know* she didn't know, because I didn't *tell* her.
MIRANDA. Well, now she knows.
RICHIE. Cause *you* told her.
MIRANDA. She deserved to know.

RICHIE.
(Quietly) What the *fuck*...

MIRANDA.
(To ROBERTA.) Let's go back to my place.

ROBERTA. Okay...

(ROBERTA and MIRANDA stand up.)

RICHIE. Wait a second. Wait.

MIRANDA. What.

RICHIE. *(To ROBERTA.)* We have to finish talking about this.

ROBERTA. We will.

MIRANDA. We need to go home now.

RICHIE. What are you going to do?

ROBERTA. I don't know.

RICHIE. Look, you have to promise me that--

ROBERTA. Okay, I promise.

RICHIE. You can't leave me dangling here. You can't do that. She tells her, and now you leave? You can't do that.

ROBERTA. I'm not doing anything.

MIRANDA. *(Overlapping with "anything".)* She won't. Okay?

RICHIE. *(To MIRANDA.)* I'm not asking you, I'm--

ROBERTA. *(To RICHIE.)* I won't talk to the police without telling you.

RICHIE. Great. Thanks. Give me a few hours notice, so I can pack my bags and be ready for when they come to string me up.

MIRANDA. Nothing's going to happen to you.

RICHIE. *(To MIRANDA.)* I'm not *asking* you.

MIRANDA. Well I'm *telling* you.

(Small pause. MIRANDA and RICHIE stare at each other.)

ROBERTA. I want to see the kid.

RICHIE. You can't do that.

ROBERTA. I won't tell anyone anything. But I need to see the kid.

RICHIE. No, no, no, no--

ROBERTA. I just need to see if he's all right.
RICHIE. You can't--
ROBERTA. And then I'll let you know.

(Small pause.)

RICHIE. You can't do this to me.
ROBERTA. I'm not.
RICHIE. Yes. You are.

(ROBERTA takes out fifty dollars and puts it on the table.)

ROBERTA. Here. Keep whatever's left.
RICHIE. You don't want to do what you're doing.
MIRANDA. *(To ROBERTA.)* Let's go.
RICHIE. Wait--
MIRANDA. We're leaving.
RICHIE. Lady--
MIRANDA. *Her name is Roberta.*

(She takes ROBERTA by the arm; they exit.)

RICHIE. Lady!

(He stares after them. He picks up the money. The WAITER emerges.)

WAITER. Is everything all right?

(RICHIE shoves the money in the WAITER's hand and exits. The WAIT-ER stares after him, looks at the money, shrugs, pockets it, and exits. Blackout.)

END OF ACT II

Act III

Scene 1

(The hospital. The ICU waiting room. GLEN is putting on his jacket. STEIN stands nearby.)

GLEN. --and you'll call me when you have some idea.

STEIN. Of course.

GLEN. Immediately.

STEIN. Yes, Mr. Provine.

GLEN. I won't be gone long.

STEIN. Okay.

GLEN. Okay. *(Small pause.)* And you're sure I can't--

STEIN. No.

GLEN. Okay. I can't put on a mask--

STEIN. No. We can't have other people in the operating room. For insurance reasons. I'm sorry.

(Small pause. GLEN nods.)

GLEN. I'm just going to walk around a little and get some air.

STEIN. Okay.

GLEN. I'll be back before he comes out, right?

STEIN. Certainly.

GLEN. When's he coming out?

STEIN. I can't say for sure but--

GLEN. Can you take a *guess?*

STEIN. --in about an hour.

GLEN. I'll make sure to be back before then. All right? I'm not going out for very long. You understand?

STEIN. I understand.

GLEN. I'm not "leaving".

STEIN. Of course not.

GLEN. I'm going to stretch my legs, get some air. Maybe I'll have a bite to eat. All I've been eating is vending machine food and cottage cheese from the nurses.

STEIN. That must be very unsatisfying.

GLEN. It is. So I'm going to get some nutrition into my body, it'll help, and then I can be on shift here with full attention. I won't nod off like I did before. You must think that's pretty irresponsible.

STEIN. Not at all. You haven't had any rest since we--

GLEN. You don't need to make excuses for me.

STEIN. I'm not.

GLEN. Call it as you see it, if it's irresponsible then call it that.

STEIN. I don't think it was irresponsible.

GLEN. *I* do.

STEIN. Okay, it's irresponsible.

GLEN. Is that right?

STEIN. Well, if you say it--

GLEN. I'd like to see *you* go through this and be perky, doctor.

STEIN. I'm not--

GLEN. You don't look so perky yourself, so don't cast stones.

STEIN. But you--

GLEN. Anyway I didn't sleep for very long, so it wasn't neglectful.

STEIN. Certainly not.

GLEN. Now I'll be back in a little.

STEIN. Yes.
GLEN. You have my phone number?
STEIN. Right here.
GLEN. You'll--
STEIN. *(Just slightly overlapping the previous line.)* I'll call.
GLEN. You will?
STEIN. Yes.

(Small pause.)

GLEN. All right. *(Small pause.)* Keep me informed.
STEIN. I will.

(Small pause.)

GLEN. I'm going.

(Small pause. He goes. STEIN sighs. Crossfade to the street corner, where THE AMAZING TARQUIN presides over a large wooden box.)

THE AMAZING TARQUIN. For my next trick, labels and generalizations, I need a volunteer--preferably one of the female persuasion. Preferably once who looks like my daughter. Oh yes--I have a daughter. *(Small pause.)* She's a gem. A gem! A precious, precious stone. *(Small pause.)* Although anyone whom I can persuade will suffice. Takers? Anybody? You, my fine lady? Or how about you? No? All right then, far be it from me to throw in the towel just yet--I've got too much left yet to clean up--*you,* sir? *(He listens to an imaginary objection from the crowd.)* But if I tell you the trick in advance, what kind of magician would I be? I'll tell you: about the same kind as I am right now...*(He listens again.)* Well how should *I* know if you're claustrophobic? Goodness gracious, friends, if you didn't trust me that much then why have you stayed here in the evening air for this long? I need a volunteer. As I've stated, a female is preferrable: it's classier, isn't it?, and more in keeping with the spirit of the--*(His head down, GLEN walks across THE AMAZING TARQUIN's circle of light.)* Ah! A wondrous wanderer, wending and winding his way! *(He steps in front of GLEN.)* My fine sir--

GLEN. Excuse me.

(GLEN circumvents THE AMAZING TARQUIN, but the magician comes around and blocks GLEN again.)

THE AMAZING TARQUIN. My fine sir, I commend you! Applaud you! Laud you!

GLEN. I'm in a hurry.

THE AMAZING TARQUIN. Not to worry. I take it as another fine element of an obviously sterling character.

GLEN. What?

THE AMAZING TARQUIN. And modest, too!

GLEN. Do you mind?

THE AMAZING TARQUIN. I would. But not currently.

GLEN. What?

THE AMAZING TARQUIN. I would mind if you left, but you haven't, so I don't. Yet.

GLEN. Yeah, well, I'm leaving now, so--

THE AMAZING TARQUIN. But you haven't even begun the trick.

GLEN. Look, asshole, get out of my way, please.

THE AMAZING TARQUIN. *(To audience.)* Ah! Even as the mouth blurts "asshole", the soul appends "please".

GLEN. That's right. Please move it, asshole.

THE AMAZING TARQUIN. Sir, I am about to conjur a fantastic reality, one you have never before imagined.

GLEN. I don't want to imagine anything. Things are bad enough as is.

THE AMAZING TARQUIN. Rough night?

GLEN. Yeah. And I don't need any--*(THE AMAZING TARQUIN steps back and gestures for GLEN to walk on. Small pause.)* Thanks. *(GLEN stares at THE AMAZING TARQUIN, then hurriedly walks toward the exit. Before he leaves, GLEN pauses, and turns back.)* Do you know anywhere around here to eat?

THE AMAZING TARQUIN. You want to *eats,* then move your *feets,* right up the *streets,* and take a *seats,* cause no place *beats*...Ruby's. Incredible edibles, one block up, turn left, red sign.

GLEN. Ruby's, huh? It's good?

THE AMAZING TARQUIN. Oh, sir--please--far be it from me to speak from no experience. I've been staking it out for months.

GLEN. But have you *eaten* there?

THE AMAZING TARQUIN. It's a sure thing. Make sure you sit near the front, look for a pretty young waitress with bags under her eyes, order the pie of the day.

GLEN. Okay. Thanks. *(Small pause. GLEN steps toward THE AMAZING TARQUIN.)* What kind of trick did you want to do?

THE AMAZING TARQUIN. My original intention was to saw a woman in half.

GLEN. A-huh.

THE AMAZING TARQUIN. A bona fide classic, more bona fide than a fourteen year-old boy during co-ed gym.

GLEN. I bet. *(Small pause.)* I'm not a woman.

THE AMAZING TARQUIN. You take what you're given, or else you're a thief. *(He bows. GLEN nods and exits. THE AMAZING TARQUIN turns to the audience.)* And for my next trick--no, lazies and jellie-molds, not a woman in half...Rather: a man in half--brought back *together!*

(He claps his hands. Crossfade to the diner. GLEN enters, looks around, and sits at the nearest booth. He picks up a menu, studies it, puts it down, and runs his hands through his hair. He presses his face into his hands, and for a moment it looks as though he is sleeping. Then he snores: he really is sleeping. OPAL approaches, pad in hand. She is distressed and trying to hide it.)

OPAL. What can I--*(She notices that GLEN is sleeping. She clears her throat to get his attention. When that doesn't work, she tries again.*

Still GLEN sleeps.) Mister. Excuse me. Mister.

(She looks offstage. She looks back at him, then offstage again. She sighs and exits. GLEN continues to sleep. Half a minute later, OPAL returns with a cup of coffee and a little bowl of cream, which she sets in front of him. He does not wake. She sighs again, then exits again. Just as she disappears, GLEN wakes.)

GLEN. *(Half asleep.)*...in, in...what?...I don't like bass fishing, I like...*(He shakes himself awake.)*...ohhh shit...*(He notices the coffee in front of him. He stares at it, confused about where it came from. He sniffs it, picks it up. Tastes it. It's too hot, and he sets it down.)* Ow ow ow go*ddammit. (He leans over and blows on the coffee. He adds a little cream, empties into the cup a sugar packet from a basket on the table, and mixes everything. He leans over and blows again, and is about to take a sip when OPAL returns with a slice of peach pie. She stops and looks at him. He doesn't see her, and is blowing on the coffee. She watches him. He picks up the cup and takes a sip. To himself.)* That's good...*(He adds more cream, sips again, slumps back in his seat with his hand on his eyes. Sighs.) Shit...*

(OPAL watches him for a moment. She is trying to decide whether to leave him be or initiate contact. She glances toward the kitchen. After a moment, she settles on stepping loudly toward him, so that he knows she's coming. He jolts awake.)

OPAL.	GLEN.
Oh! Sorry!	What the...

OPAL. I'm sorry. I'm sorry, I'm so sorry...I apologize for that, I didn't...but you were asleep, and--

GLEN. Yeah.

OPAL. I thought...you might...But maybe not, I'll just--*(She starts to exit.)* I'll be back in a minute for your order...

GLEN. *(Overlapping "for your order.")* Wait wait wait, hang on. Hang on! *(OPAL turns back.)* It's okay. I'm not supposed to be asleep anyway.

OPAL. I should've asked myself first if I'd like it if someone woke me up like that. I'd say no, obviously, and then I would've known not to do it to you. But, I don't always think that way.

GLEN. Hey, young lady, relax.

OPAL. Okay. Sorry.

GLEN. I'm just stopping in. I'm picking up food. I sat down at the booth to rest my legs and I fell asleep. But I can't afford to be asleep right now, so it's a good thing you woke me up. *(Small pause.)* I mean it.

(Small pause.)

OPAL. ...okay.

GLEN. There ya go.

OPAL. All right, well...then, what can I do for you...?

GLEN. I need...*(He looks down.)* I was gonna ask for some coffee.

OPAL. Oh.

GLEN. But I need it to go.

OPAL. Okay. Sorry.

GLEN. And...two pieces of...what is that, peach?

(OPAL looks down, seems to be surprised that she's holding the pie.)

OPAL. Uh...yes.

GLEN. Okay, to go.

OPAL. Right. I'll...okay...*(Flustered, she takes the coffee and pie and goes off. A moment later she returns with a styrofoam cup and a container for the pie.)* I'm sorry, I'm tired, I hope I...here you go...

GLEN. Thank you. What do I owe you?

(OPAL totals the check while GLEN looks inside the container.)

OPAL. Uh...four...fifty.

GLEN. *(Overlapping with "fifty".)* Sorry, but I need two.

OPAL. What?

GLEN. There's only one piece of pie in here. I asked for two, I'm bringing it for a friend.

OPAL. Oh...sorry...*(She glances offstage.)* That might be...uh...the last of it. Hang on. *(She runs off. GLEN sighs, checks his watch. She returns.)* That one's out but he's baking another right now.

GLEN. How long will it take?

OPAL. He said about twenty minutes.

GLEN. Oh, man, you're kidding...

OPAL. I'm sorry, I'm really sorry, but--

GLEN. You know what, you can just--what else is there...

(He picks up the menu.)

OPAL.	GLEN.
I can--mister, if you--	Okay, how about a...

OPAL. I can bring it to you.

GLEN. How about aaaa--*(He looks up.)*--what's that?

OPAL. I can bring it to you. It'll be done twenty minutes, I'll just bring it on by, if you're close. Or--even if you're not. It's okay, I don't mind, I feel bad that...it's good pie, I'm sure your friend will like it.

GLEN. Don't you have to--I mean, you can't just leave in the middle of--

OPAL. I'm off. I'm not even supposed to be here now. My shift ended a while ago, but I...I came back, I thought I'd work some...some more, some...*overtime.* I needed to get away, and so, I thought...but I'm tired, and it was a bad idea. I'm going home anyway, and I'd be happy to...to...*(Small pause.)* It's no big deal.

(Pause. GLEN appraises her.)

GLEN. You know the hospital up the street?

(Small pause.)

OPAL. Yes.

GLEN. It's the ICU. First floor, you can come in through the emergency room doors.

OPAL. Okay.

GLEN. Or go to the front desk, they'll show you where to go.

OPAL. Okay.

GLEN. Okay. *(Small pause. He gets up.)* Thanks.

OPAL. You're welcome.

(They look at each other for a moment.)

GLEN. Ah, hang on...

(He fishes out his wallet.)

OPAL. No, it's okay.

GLEN. Come on--

OPAL. Mister, I can--don't worry about it.

GLEN. I've got food I'm taking out here, someone's got to pay for it, and it's not going to be you.

OPAL. I'll--

GLEN. No, sorry, no way.

OPAL. You can pay me later.

GLEN. When?

OPAL. When I bring the food by. You can pay me then. *(Small pause. GLEN puts his wallet away.)* Thank you.

(Small pause.)

GLEN. I'll be there.

OPAL. Give me about a half an hour.

GLEN. Okay.

OPAL. I'll bring fresh pieces, you don't have to worry about that one. I mean, you can keep that, too, but, I'll bring two new pieces. *(Small pause.)* It's good pie. You'll...you'll like it. *(Small pause.)* Everybody does.

GLEN. I'm sure I will.

(He looks at her, and exits. She stares after him. Blackout.)

Scene 2

(The hospital. ICU waiting room. MIRANDA, ROBERTA, and STEIN are standing.)

STEIN. Then what exactly *is* the nature of--

MIRANDA. It's hard to explain.

STEIN. Can you try and...?

MIRANDA. It's a private matter.

STEIN. Miss, I am sorry, I am very sorry. It is not my choice to let you in or not. There are a lot of legal issues involved here.

MIRANDA. Like what.

STEIN. For one, it's an issue of security.

MIRANDA. You think we're going to *do* something?

STEIN. I am not saying that you would, per se. But you must understand, we can't let anybody into the ICU who wants to come in. Sometimes there are people here because other people *tried* to do something to them.

MIRANDA. We're not going to shoot him. You know that, right? Look at us?

STEIN. Okay, but--

MIRANDA. You can frisk us if you want.

STEIN. It's a rule. If a rule is not applied in equal measure then it's not much of a rule.

MIRANDA. *(Annoyed)* Don't tell me what a rule is, I know what a rule is, I went to kindergarten--

ROBERTA. *(Jumping in; gently.)* What if we just want to know his name? Can you tell us that?

STEIN. Not exactly.

ROBERTA. His first name?

STEIN. Ma'am, no, I'm sorry, but no. There are legal questions, questions of privacy, doctor-patient privilege, that I would be violating if...I mean, we're not allowed to release that information to anybody who walks in here.

MIRANDA. We're not anybody.

STEIN. I am sure you're not, but--

MIRANDA. We have a connection to him.

STEIN. You do, okay then, what--

MIRANDA. *(Overlapping with "okay then".)* Yes, we, we're, we're here from his church. We're the goodwill society from his, his church.

(Small pause.)

STEIN. You don't know his name.

MIRANDA. It's a very large church.

STEIN. Ma'am, please, I've got get back inside, and--

ROBERTA. Can we wait around until his father comes back?

STEIN. I would appreciate it if--well, okay, *fine:* you can wait in the lobby.

ROBERTA. All right.

STEIN. I don't know how long it's going to be.

ROBERTA. We'll wait.

STEIN. *(To ROBERTA.)* I appreciate it.

ROBERTA. Thank you.

(STEIN starts off.)

MIRANDA. What if I told you I hit him.

(Pause. STEIN turns around.)

STEIN. Pardon?

MIRANDA. Then would you let us in?

STEIN.
Excuse me--*what?*

ROBERTA.
(To MIRANDA, sotto voce.) What are you saying?

MIRANDA. I hit him. That's our connection. Can you let us in now?

ROBERTA.
What are you saying!

MIRANDA.
I hit him. He was on his bike. I wasn't looking and I hit him.

STEIN . You really shouldn't joke about that--

MIRANDA.
I'm not joking.

ROBERTA.
(To MIRANDA.) Please shut up.

MIRANDA. I'm not joking. He was wearing--

ROBERTA.
Stop it!

MIRANDA.
(Louder than ROBERTA.)--he was wearing a blue shirt.

ROBERTA. Excuse us.
STEIN. *(To MIRANDA.)* Ma'am--

ROBERTA.
We're very sorry about this.

MIRANDA.
(Louder than ROBERTA.) With a flag. The shirt had a flag on it.

STEIN. *(Coming closer.)*What?
MIRANDA. A flag.

(ROBERTA tries to pull MIRANDA off.)

ROBERTA. Excuse us, we have--
STEIN. Wait--wait a minute--

ROBERTA.
We have to go--

MIRANDA.
I didn't report it. I need to see him. I need to see if he's all right.

STEIN. That's not something you should, uh, uh, *joke* about, because there are very serious--

ROBERTA.
We know. We're sorry. *(To MIRANDA.)* Say you're sorry and stop joking around with--

MIRANDA.
I'm not joking. I saw the flag. Right? He was wearing a blue t-shirt with a flag.

STEIN. If that--oh Jesus...if that's the, the *case*, then--

ROBERTA.   MIRANDA.

It is *not* the case!   It is absolutely the case.

STEIN. We need to figure out, I need to--you need to call the--*(He turns around.)* Nurse, please call security. Hello? Is there a nurse here? Nurse?

(He continues calling for a nurse as MIRANDA and ROBERTA talk. Their speeches should be timed so that they end at about the same time. The whole time ROBERTA struggles to clamp her hand over MIRANDA's mouth. As their fighting grows more intense, STEIN notices and begins calling for "security", moving frantically when his cries are not answered.)

MIRANDA.

I didn't know what to do. I was late for work. I was scared and I barely even realized he was there, I didn't know what to do. It was like it was happening to someone else. I felt like I had given my hands to someone else and that they were doing it instead of me, but I couldn't stand it and I've been calling around to hospitals all morning. Because it's all my fault. Everything is all my fault. I need to know if he's okay. Even if he isn't okay, I need to know that. I'm not a bad person but sometimes things happen and you find yourself at the helm of them, whether you want to or not. But now I'm ready to see him and to figure out what I'm supposed to do.

ROBERTA.

Shut up. Shut up. Shut up! Stop it! Shut up! Shut up. Stop talking. Stop it. Stop it stop it stop it stop it shut--shut up! Shut up! *Shut up! Will you shut up! Will you shut the fuck up! Shut the fuck up! Shut up! Shut up! You can't do this, shut up! Why are you doing this? Why are you-- shut up! Shut up! STOP IT! STOP! STOP! SHUT UP! SHUT YOUR FUCKING MOUTH! YOU STUPID BITCH WILL YOU SHUT YOUR FUCKING MOUTH, SHUT UP SHUT UP SHUT UP SHUT UP!*

(ROBERTA slaps MIRANDA, hard. MIRANDA falls to the ground. ROBERTA runs from the hospital. After a moment, MIRANDA sits up.)

STEIN. *(Very shaken.)* Ma'am--

MIRANDA. It...it wasn't me. It was...I just said that...I said it so we could get in.

STEIN. Ma'am--

MIRANDA. I didn't mean it. I'm sorry. It was just a joke. I didn't mean it. *(She gets up.)* I...I have to go...

STEIN. *(Very shaken.)* Ma'am, you need to--to--you can't--I am, as a doctor, I am *forbidding* you to--you need to, to, to, to *sit* down, and, and, and, and *wait* right there, because this is *not* what you were, were *talking* about before, this is an entirely different circumstance, and it is not within my authority to--*(MIRANDA starts to walk off.)* Ma'am, stop. Stop. Stop, Ma'am. Ma'am! *Ma'am! You can't--(MIRANDA is gone.)* STOP! MA'AM! I *order* you to--*(Turns around.) IS THERE A FUCK-ING NURSE IN THIS PLACE!*

(Blackout.)

Scene 3

(The streetcorner. THE AMAZING TARQUIN holds two large silver rings.)

THE AMAZING TARQUIN. Ring ring! Ring ring! Operator will you connect--connect--I said--*(ROBERTA, crying, comes running across the stage. TARQUIN watches her as she crosses and exits. A brief pause. He looks at the audience.)* Ahem. As I was saying--

(MIRANDA comes running after ROBERTA.)

MIRANDA. *Wait!*

(MIRANDA crosses and exits. Another pause. TARQUIN faces the audience.)

THE AMAZING TARQUIN. Of all the adverse circumstances under which I have performed, these, latelys and johnnycomes, are the absolute adverst. Now. As I was saying--

(MIRANDA comes running back on. Now she sees TARQUIN, and runs up to him.)

MIRANDA. Excuse me. Have you seen a lady in a business suit run past here? *(MIRANDA points offstage.)* Coming from the direction of the hospital. Crying, probably.
THE AMAZING TARQUIN. Indeed. I have indeed.
MIRANDA. You did! Where'd she go?
THE AMAZING TARQUIN. I'll tell you--*(He wields the silver rings.)*--but first, a metaphor.
MIRANDA. What?
THE AMAZING TARQUIN. Observe carefully.
MIRANDA. I don't have time for this.

(She turns to exit. As she does, ROBERTA appears on the other side of the stage. Silence. TARQUIN holds the rings up, and touches them together. As he does, a single, clear bell rings out. Slowly, MIRANDA and ROBERTA begin to walk toward one another. The bell resounds, fading as they approaches one another. They stop a few feet apart, and the bell fades out. Pause.)

ROBERTA. I'm leaving.
MIRANDA. Please don't.
ROBERTA. I have to. You made me. *(Small pause.)* Why did you do that.
MIRANDA. I thought--I don't know. Please don't--*(She laughs,*

puts a hand on her forehead. TARQUIN slowly brings the first ring toward the second ring.)--I can't believe I'm saying this: please don't leave.

ROBERTA. Why the fuck did you--don't you have any impulse control?

MIRANDA. I guess not.

ROBERTA. That was such a stupid thing to do, Miranda.

MIRANDA. I know. *(Small pause.)* Please don't be mad.

ROBERTA. I'm mad.

(Small pause. TARQUIN stops moving the first ring; the two rings are now a few inches apart.)

MIRANDA. I thought you wanted to check up on him.

ROBERTA. Yes. That's exactly what I wanted to do. *Check up on him.* Not confess to the emergency room doctor.

MIRANDA. You didn't confess, I did.

(As ROBERTA says the next lines, TARQUIN slowly moves the second ring away from the first ring.)

ROBERTA. *I know, I saw.*

MIRANDA. It made sense to me. It still makes sense, somewhere, to me.

ROBERTA. How you thought that was going to make me feel better--or him, or anyone--how you thought it was going to be an improvement--I don't understand.

MIRANDA. I know what you wanted.

ROBERTA. No you don't.

MIRANDA. You had to tell someone.

ROBERTA. *I* had to tell someone. Not you.

MIRANDA. I did it for--

ROBERTA. Oh Jesus, don't--don't--don't say that.

MIRANDA. I did.

ROBERTA. You don't even know me.

MIRANDA. Yes I do.

ROBERTA. You don't know me, I don't know you.

MIRANDA. You do know me, you know more about me than--

ROBERTA. *No.*

(TARQUIN stops moving the second ring. Pause.)

MIRANDA. Okay. *(Small pause.)* I'm sorry.

(Pause)

ROBERTA. I'm not sure it's up to me. I mean, you're the one in trouble, now.

MIRANDA. I want you to forgive me.

ROBERTA. But it's not up to me.

MIRANDA. I want you to say that you forgive me.

(Small pause as they stare at one another. MIRANDA walks toward ROBERTA and embraces her. As this happens, TARQUIN brings the rings together, so that they overlap like one ring. ROBERTA eventually puts her arms around MIRANDA. Small pause. The hug breaks, and TARQUIN slowly passes the rings apart; they have now become interlocked.)

ROBERTA. I admire you.

MIRANDA. What for?

ROBERTA. You just do things. It's like you don't even think about them.

MIRANDA. I do think about them. Afterwards.

ROBERTA. Did you think about coming to the hotel?

MIRANDA. I haven't thought about it yet.

ROBERTA. Not yet?

MIRANDA. No. I will.

ROBERTA. All I could do was think about it while it was happening.

MIRANDA. What were you thinking?

ROBERTA. I was embarrassed because I forgot to shave my legs.

(MIRANDA smiles.)

MIRANDA. I like your legs.

ROBERTA. Thank you. We shouldn't stand here. They might be looking for us right now.

MIRANDA. Shit.

ROBERTA. Yes.

MIRANDA. We could run somewhere.

ROBERTA. I don't know if that's a good idea.

MIRANDA. Then what are we going to do?

ROBERTA. I'm leaving.

MIRANDA. Leaving Dallas.

ROBERTA. I'm leaving Dallas and I'm going back to where I'm from.

(MIRANDA looks questioningly at ROBERTA, who glances down uncomfortably. TARQUIN spins one ring inside the other.)

MIRANDA. You're not going to tell me? *(ROBERTA is silent.)* I think it would be helpful if you told me where you wanted to go. Not to mention polite. *(Small pause.)* I'd like a say in the matter.

(Small pause. ROBERTA looks up.)

ROBERTA. I don't think we should go together. *(Small pause.)* First of all, we could be in a lot of trouble. You could be. I could--I don't even want to think about it. But it's much worse if we're together. *(Small pause.)* This is not like Thelma and Louise.

(Small pause.)

MIRANDA. What about the kid? *(Small pause.)* This morning you were burning up with guilt.

ROBERTA. I know. *(Small pause.)* I'm not, anymore. *(Small pause.)* The doctor said it. He said: you're not a *friend,* you're not a *relative,* you're not *anything* to this person. *(Small pause.)* He's right.

MIRANDA. Aren't you worried about him?

ROBERTA. Of course. But that doesn't make it my fault.

(Small pause.)

MIRANDA. That's what I told you this morning.

ROBERTA. Yes.

MIRANDA. You didn't listen to me then.

ROBERTA. No.

(Small pause.)

MIRANDA. You can understand why this is a little frustrating, can't you? I mean, now I'm in a big mess, and you just should've listened to me.

ROBERTA. I'm sorry.

(Small pause. MIRANDA sighs.)

MIRANDA. Whatever. Forget it.

ROBERTA. At least I learned something.

(Small pause, then MIRANDA bursts out laughing.)

MIRANDA. You know what I was before I was in travel?

ROBERTA. You were a waitress.

MIRANDA. Right, but after that and before travel--I was a nursery teacher. *(She laughs.)* I thought I wanted to teach.

ROBERTA. Why did you stop?

MIRANDA. I wasn't a very good teacher. Or--I don't know. Maybe the kids learned something, and I couldn't see it. Maybe the importance of whatever, math, will only become apparent to them twenty years down the line. *(She laughs.)* I really hope so. I had a headache for two years. *(She laughs again, shakes her head.)* You probably can't believe that, can you.

(ROBERTA nods. Small pause.)

ROBERTA. *(Softly)* I hate this town. I never wanted to live here. My ex-husband wanted to live here. *(Small pause. ROBERTA looks at MIRANDA.)* Did you know that?

MIRANDA. No. *(Small pause.)* Tell me something else. *(Silence)* I want to know something about you. *(Silence)* What are we going to do?

(Silence)

ROBERTA. I'll miss you. *(MIRANDA shakes her head.)* I will.

MIRANDA. Okay.

ROBERTA. Thank you.

MIRANDA. This was pretty fast, huh?

ROBERTA. Yes.

MIRANDA. That doesn't make a difference to me, you know. Everything for me has gone fast. This is just as important as--*(ROBERTA placed her fingers on MIRANDA's lips. Then ROBERTA leans in and gently kisses MIRANDA. Pause.)* We should get going. *(Small pause.)* Or...I should get going. *(Long pause.)* All right. *(Small pause.)* You should get going, too, you know. Back to wherever it is you come from. You don't have to tell me, but you should follow your own advice and get the hell out of this town.

ROBERTA. I will. *(Pause. MIRANDA starts to walk away.)* Hold on.

(MIRANDA turns around. Small pause. THE AMAZING TARQUIN slowly, silently begins to pull at the rings, as though to separate them.)

MIRANDA. What.

ROBERTA. I need a favor. *(Small pause.)* I want to walk away.

(Small pause.)

MIRANDA. What?

ROBERTA. I want you to stay there.

MIRANDA. This is a lot to ask of me, you know. First you...and then--*(She breaks off, and emits a short, sudden sob. She inhales sharply and pulls herself together.)* Okay.

ROBERTA. I'm sorry for asking. You don't have to.

MIRANDA. It's okay. (Small pause.) I'll wait.

(Small pause. Neither of them move.)

ROBERTA. I'm sorry...

MIRANDA. It's okay.

(Small pause. Neither of them move.)

ROBERTA. I've never done this before. Usually I'm you. You being you in this situation.

MIRANDA. I got it.

ROBERTA. Okay. *(Small pause.)* This is hard.

MIRANDA. Take your time. I'll wait here. *(MIRANDA struggles not to cry. Smiling.)* I'll see what it's like.

ROBERTA. You won't like it.

(MIRANDA half-laughs, half-sobs.)

MIRANDA. How will I know until I've tried?

ROBERTA. Trust me on this. *(Small pause.)* Just trust me.

(Long pause. ROBERTA turns and exits. As she does, TARQUIN separates the rings, dropping one ring to the floor. The ring rolls to cen-

ter stage and falls over. Crying, MIRANDA stares after ROBERTA, then exits. A brief pause. The lights narrow on the ring and on TAR-QUIN. RICHIE enters, looking like hell. He spots the the ring, and stares at it for a moment before going to pick it up. He holds it, stares at it.)

THE AMAZING TARQUIN. Ring ring. *(Startled, RICHIE looks up and sees TARQUIN.)* Where are you headed, Taxi-Man? *(RICHIE stares at TARQUIN suspiciously.)* Your badge?
    RICHIE. Oh.
    THE AMAZING TARQUIN. It would appear that you *do* need some stinkin badges. *(Small pause. RICHIE seems unsure of what to make of TARQUIN.)* You were saying?
    RICHIE. What?
    THE AMAZING TARQUIN. Your destination, sir, in our destined nation. Your goal. Whence you will come when you leave the place to which you are currently headstronging toward, and I'd end there except I hate ending on a preposition. *(Small pause.)* Where are you going?

(Small pause.)

    RICHIE. I--*(Small pause.)* The diner.
    THE AMAZING TARQUIN. Hungry?
    RICHIE. I need matches.

(TARQUIN immediately produces the torch from his first scene, and sets it ablaze. RICHIE leaps back, staring at it.)

    THE AMAZING TARQUIN. Go on, try it, try it, you'll see, you'll get all the fire proof that it's as good as any in the world. *(After a beat, RICHIE takes out a pack of cigarettes, and approaches TARQUIN. RICHIE hesitates, and TARQUIN smiles. RICHIE tenatively lights the cigarette using the flame of the torch. He smokes.)* There, now wasn't that nice? *(RICHIE nods.)* Now there's no need to go to the diner, although if you're hungry as a horse you could always chow down. Life is trough, and there's no better panacea than pie. But before you go-- eh...

(TARQUIN glances at the ring, which RICHIE is still holding. RICHIE follows his gaze.)

RICHIE. Sorry--is this--

THE AMAZING TARQUIN. No no, keep it, all yours, I just wanted you to know that you had it.

(TARQUIN bows. RICHIE looks at the ring, then at the cigarette.)

RICHIE. Which way's the hospital? *(TARQUIN points offstage.)* Thanks.

(RICHIE exits. TARQUIN tosses the remaining ring into the air. It does not come down. He smiles. Blackout.)

Scene 4

(The hospital. The ICU waiting room. GLEN and STEIN.)

GLEN. *What do you mean she walked out!*
STEIN. I don't know, I don't know, I tried to--

(GLEN grabs STEIN.)

GLEN. Aren't your parents a little *pissed off* that they spent all that money to send you through *medical school* and you still don't know a goddamn thing?

STEIN. *(Exhausted) Oh shit...*

GLEN. *(Shaking STEIN.)* The woman that mowed down my kid comes in and offers herself to you on a *platter* and you *escort* her to the door?

STEIN. I tried to stop her, I called for security...

GLEN. And?

STEIN. Nobody came.

GLEN. Then why didn't you go after her yourself? Why didn't you run after her and *tackle* her? Huh? Why not!

STEIN. Oh Jesus...

GLEN. Why not! *Why not! (GLEN shakes STEIN. STEIN moans. GLEN releases STEIN. STEIN falls down.)* Jesus fucking Christ...

(STEIN crawls to a chair.)

STEIN. I am not a, a, a *vigilante.*

GLEN. Did you call the police.

STEIN. They asked me what she looked like and they said they'd send someone over when they had someone.

GLEN. Did they...did they put out a--a *report* on her? Are they looking for her?

STEIN. They told me they can't, she's not a criminal.

GLEN. She *is* a criminal!

STEIN. Call them up and tell them that.

GLEN. I will. I will!

STEIN. It's not going to do any good.

GLEN. Yes it will.

STEIN. We should just wait here.

GLEN. No, we should not "just wait here", we should get off our asses and go phone the police.

STEIN. Fine.

(GLEN storms from the room. STEIN leans his head back against the wall and falls asleep. After a moment, OPAL enters. She is holding a large brown paper bag. She looks around, looks at STEIN. She doesn't know what to do, so she sits down. After a moment GLEN storms back in.)

GLEN. Somebody's on the fucking pho--

(He leaps back when he sees OPAL, banging into STEIN.)

STEIN.	GLEN.
(Waking up.) Ahhhhhh!	*(To OPAL.)* Oh my gosh, I'm sorry, miss.

OPAL. *(Leaping up.)* That's okay.

GLEN. I didn't know you were here.

STEIN.	OPAL.
(Dazed) Wha...jesus...	I just got here.

GLEN. It's--it's very rude of me to come running in here like that. I apologize.

OPAL. There's no need.

GLEN. And excuse my language.

OPAL. It's fine.

(STEIN stands up.)

STEIN. Hello, excuse me, hello. Can I help you?

OPAL. I'm here--

GLEN. This young lady was kind enough to deliver me food.

STEIN. I see. What?

GLEN. She's--

OPAL. I'm from the diner.

STEIN. Oh.

GLEN. *(To STEIN.)* Someone's on the phone. I couldn't call. I'll call in a minute. *(To OPAL.)* I'm in the middle of something, right now.

OPAL. I'm sorry--

GLEN. No no no no no. You don't have to apologize for...for... anything. *(He stands looking at her. Quietly.)* You came here...

OPAL. Yes.

(Small pause.)

GLEN. That's...that's...*(Small pause.)* I have to--I have to make a phone call.

OPAL. I'll just leave the pie--

GLEN. No. Please. Sit down for--wait a second. I'll be back in one second. *(To STEIN, who is rubbing his eyes.)* Stay here and keep her company.

STEIN. What? *(GLEN exits. STEIN looks at OPAL.)* Did I fall asleep?

OPAL. You were asleep when I came in.

STEIN. I...*(Small pause.)* I don't know what's going on. *(OPAL nods.)* Thank you.

OPAL. You're welcome.

(STEIN notices her bag.)

STEIN. What is that?

OPAL. Pie.

STEIN. Pie...

OPAL. It's for...I don't know his name. He ordered it. It wasn't ready.

STEIN. So you brought it here? *(OPAL nods.)* That's very nice of you.

OPAL. I'm on my way home.

STEIN. You live near here?

OPAL. Not really.

STEIN. Then how is it on your way home.

OPAL. If I go a couple miles out of my way...*(Small pause.)* Then it's right on the way.

(Small pause.)

STEIN. Aha.

OPAL. It's not very...um...*scientific.*

STEIN. Not really, no.

OPAL. I've never been good at science.

STEIN. Neither have I.

OPAL. But you're a doctor.

STEIN. I know.

OPAL. Then what do you do, if you don't do science?

STEIN. To tell you the truth, I have absolutely no idea. *(Small pause.)* Excuse me.

(He exits. OPAL stares after him. A moment later, GLEN enters.)

GLEN. Where'd he go?

OPAL. I don't know. He just left.

GLEN. Don't mind him. He's like that.

OPAL. Here's your pie. I brought some extra, and some extra coffee. No charge, Ruby said.

GLEN. Thanks. Thanks a lot.

OPAL. Don't thank me, it's Ruby's place.

GLEN. Thank Ruby then.

OPAL. I'll tell her when I go back to work.

GLEN. I thought you were going home.

OPAL. I am, now. But I have to go back to work at some point.

GLEN. What do I owe you?

OPAL. Eight twenty-five. That's for two pieces, and one coffee.

(GLEN gets his wallet out and gives her ten dollars. She starts to make change from her purse when he stops her.)

GLEN. Delivery charge.

OPAL. It's really fine, I--

GLEN. It's a tip.

(Small pause.)

OPAL. All right. Thanks.

GLEN. It was very nice of you to come over here.

(OPAL smiles wearily at him, then starts to exit. She turns at the door.)

OPAL. Did you make your phone call?

(Small pause.)

GLEN. No. I didn't.
OPAL. Is everything okay?
GLEN. Yeah.
OPAL. Oh. Why not?

(Long pause.)

GLEN. I thought I'd do somebody a favor.
OPAL. Oh.

(Small pause.)

GLEN. I owe this person a kick in the ass, pardon my French. But...it doesn't matter. *(He laughs.)* Even if they were here, I don't know if I'd care to give it to them. *(Small pause. He looks at her.)* I've been in this hospital too long. It doesn't help your sanity. Look at the doctor. *(She smiles.)* Naww, you're right, he's okay. Maybe I'll give him some pie if there's enough.
OPAL. I hope so.
GLEN. Yeah. *(Small pause.)* You want some pie?
OPAL. No thanks. I've had...plenty.
GLEN. You sure? *(She smiles and nods. Small pause.)* Thank you. Very much.
OPAL. You're welcome. You try and have a nice day.
GLEN. I will. You too. *(She smiles at him and exits. He looks in the bag. He extracts its contents: two cups of coffee and an entire pie. He looks at the pie, shakes his head. He sets it down on one of the waiting room tables and unwraps it. He smells it and smiles. He reaches into the bag and takes out some plastic cutlery, some napkins, a small paper*

plate. He is cutting himself a piece when RICHIE enters, holding the silver ring. He glances around and sees GLEN. GLEN notices RICHIE. Pause.) You here for someone? *(RICHIE nods.)* The doctor's busy. I'm Glen. Come in and have some pie. *(RICHIE stares at GLEN, then looks out the door.)* He'll be back in a minute, I promise. *(RICHIE looks at GLEN.)* It's good. It's fresh. I just had it delivered.

(Small pause.)

> RICHIE. What kind is it?
> GLEN. Peach.

(Small pause.)

> RICHIE. Peach?
> GLEN. Mm-hm. *(Small pause.)* Hey, look, I'm sorry. If you don't want to, you don't have to come in. I've been here a while and I'm feeling like part of the wallpaper. Pretty soon they're going to have to peel me off and put me in the shower. All I know is, when I came in here, nobody offered me any pie, and I wish they had. *(Small pause. RICHIE comes over, sits a few chairs away from GLEN.)* There you go. Cut you a piece? *(RICHIE nods.)* Okay.

(GLEN cuts RICHIE a piece of pie.)

> RICHIE. Thanks.
> GLEN. You look like you've had a night. *(RICHIE nods.)* I won't ask. It's none of my business.
> RICHIE. Thanks.
> GLEN. You want me to shut up? *(RICHIE shakes his head.)* If you do, just say so. *(RICHIE nods. Referring to the ring.)* Heck is that? *(RICHIE looks at the ring. He seems not to know what to do with it. After a beat, RICHIE holds the ring out to GLEN, who takes it. GLEN examines the ring.)* Is this a--what is this? *(GLEN glances up at RICHIE, who shakes his head: "I don't know". GLEN turns the ring*

over in his hand, then suddenly laughs and holds it over his head like a halo.) See? *(GLEN laughs again. RICHIE smiles.)* Ahhh, fuck it...*(GLEN holds the ring back out to RICHIE.)* Here, give it a try. It'll make you feel better. *(Small pause.)* Go on. *(After a beat, RICHIE takes hold of the ring. He holds it, looks at it, then at GLEN. GLEN nods at RICHIE. RICHIE holds the ring over his head. GLEN laughs.)* Man, if we got you a harp, you'd be all set.

(He laughs. RICHIE smiles, then hands the ring out to GLEN.)

RICHIE. Here.
GLEN. What.
RICHIE. Please.

(After a beat, GLEN takes the ring. RICHIE holds on to it for one moment, and the two men look at each other, each grasping the ring. Then RICHIE lets go, and GLEN takes the ring. GLEN smiles at it, then jokingly--briefly--puts it back over his head. He laughs, and RICHIE smiles. GLEN puts the ring on his lap, and turns his attention to his pie.)

GLEN . I don't know where the doctor's got to. He just wandered off. I guess there's things he needs to do, he's a doctor. I've been chewing his ass for a while but he really should be in there attending to...patients. *(GLEN takes a bite of pie.)* Mmmm. She wasn't kidding. This is good. *(He eats some more, then puts his fork down, and cuts two pieces of pie, roots around in the paper bag, finds some wax paper, and wraps the two pieces in it.)* I'm gonna set aside a couple of pieces. It's my son's favorite. He'll appreciate it when he wakes up. *(RICHIE stirs nervously. GLEN looks at him.)* Your son's--? *(RICHIE shakes his head.)* A-huh. *(Small pause.)* I won't ask. It's none of my business. *(RICHIE nods.)* My son's in there. *(RICHIE and GLEN stare at each other for a moment. Then GLEN looks at RICHIE's plate.)* You didn't eat anything.
    RICHIE. I'm not hungry. Right now.

GLEN. Maybe you'll get hungry.

RICHIE. Maybe.

GLEN. You can save it for later, I don't mind.

RICHIE. Thanks.

GLEN. Don't thank me, thank...whoever it is, I don't remember the name of the place. *(GLEN takes a bite, chews in silence. RICHIE watches him. RICHIE takes a deep breath, closes his eyes. He starts taking deep breaths, one after another. Out of the corner of his eye, GLEN notices RICHIE taking deep breaths. GLEN raises his eyebrows at it, stares at it, shakes his head, and goes back to eating pie. RICHIE takes a few final deep breaths and opens his eyes. He stands up and looks at GLEN.)* Feel better?

(Small pause.)

RICHIE. Listen...

(Small pause. As RICHIE opens his mouth to speak, STEIN enters, his eyes wide.)

STEIN. Mr. Provine--*(GLEN and RICHIE turn to face STEIN.)* Dewey's awake. *(Small pause. GLEN grabs the wax-paper-wrapped pie, and bolts from the room. The ring falls to the floor. STEIN looks at it, bends, and picks it up. He stares at it for a moment, then passes his hand through it. He stares at his hand, wiggles his fingers, wondering at them. Then he realizes what he's doing, and that RICHIE seems to be waiting for him. STEIN straightens up and clears his throat.)* Uh, can I help you?

RICHIE. I needed to speak to him.

STEIN. Oh. *(STEIN turns around, looking after GLEN.)* I'm sure it can wait. *(Small pause. STEIN squints at the pie.)* Is that peach?

(Blackout.)

Scene 5

(The street corner. THE AMAZING TARQUIN. He holds a large, black, velvet drawstring bag.)

THE AMAZING TARQUIN. Ladies and gentlemen! Your attention is appreciated. My bag of tricks is almost empty, but it still feels pretty heavy. That's because interest is compounding! And speaking of pounding, your poor heads! Enough of this malarky! Hogwash! Diddle-daddle! Stuff-and-nonsense! Enough I say! Enough! *(Small pause. He smiles.)* Almost enough. There's still my final magical gesture, the disbursal and disappearance of all slippery things. *(He turns to face the opposite side of the stage. OPAL enters, walking with her bag slung over her shoulder.)* Young lady!

(OPAL stops in a circle of light, separated from him by most of the width of the stage.)

OPAL. Yes?

THE AMAZING TARQUIN. Young lady...

OPAL. Yes...? *(Pause as he looks at her.)* Did you say something, mister?

THE AMAZING TARQUIN. I just wanted to get a good look at you.

(She takes a step back.)

OPAL. You're not one of those old perv guys, are you?

THE AMAZING TARQUIN. "Old perv guys"? But no, my fair maiden. Merely an appreciator of the things that...an a--an a--appreciator of--

(He is having trouble with the words.)

OPAL. Are you all right?

THE AMAZING TARQUIN. *(Weakly)*...yes. Yes. I am...certainly that.

OPAL. You sounded a little...sick.

THE AMAZING TARQUIN. No. It's not that. It's something else. *(Small pause.)* You look so beautiful, it struck me dumb.
(OPAL smiles despite herself.)

OPAL. Yeah.

(Small pause. He holds up the bag.)

THE AMAZING TARQUIN. This is for you.
OPAL. Me? *(He nods.)* What is it?
THE AMAZING TARQUIN. Your inheritence.
OPAL. What?

(He places the bag on the ground, then exits. Small pause. After a moment, OPAL walks to the bag. She stares at it, then looks off, after him. She looks around, trying to decide what to do. Slowly, she kneels beside it and opens it up. She looks inside and gasps. Pause. She reaches in, and slowly takes out a handful of precious stones: opals. She puts them on the ground, and takes out another handful. And another. And another, more and more quickly. Gems pile around her. She shakes the bag out. Hundreds of gems spill out. OPAL looks offstage after him. Brief pause, then: blackout.)

END OF PLAY

Property plot

Act I, scene 2

"Torch to flower" magic trick (or "match to flower")

Act I, scene 3
A peach pie
Plastic cups
Knife
Hand towel

Act I, scene 4

Bicycle helmet

Act I, scene 5
Coffee cup with hot coffee

Act I, scene 6

Vase of flowers
Clipboard

Act I, scene 7

Empty pie tray

Act I, scene 8

Burn kit

Act I, scene 9

"Blank card deck" magic trick

Act I, scene 10

Pocket-pack of tissues

Act I, scene 11

Two slices of peach pie
Two forks
Beeper

Act II, scene 1

"Coin into hat" magic trick

Act II, scene 2

Four menus
Fruit plate
Omelette
$50 bill

Act III, scene 1

Large wooden box
Coffee, creamer, sugar
Slice of peach pie
Styrofoam container

Act III, scene 3

"Rings" magic trick
Cigarettes

Act III, scene 4

Large brown paper bag
$10 bill
Styrofoam coffee cups
Plastic forks
Paper plates
Whole peach pie

Act III, scene 5

Black velvet bag with opals

ADULT ENTERTAINMENT
Elaine May

There is a cloud over porn queen Heidi the Ho's cable TV show. Her guests are mourning the passing of their employer and mentor, a legendary porn film maker. Tired of working for others, this motley group of adult video veterans decides to write and shoot their own extravaganza, an art film. Script one doesn't live up to their expectations so they bring in a new writer, one who insists they read the classics to prepare for their roles. Unexpected light bulbs go off and hilarity escalates. "May's best work … surprises us with humanity in the midst of the ridiculous.... It's the comedy of the year."— *New York Post*. "Only a frenzied comic mind could imagine ... this delight ... with its giddy, raunchy sense of humor."—*Show Business Weekly*. 3 m., 3 f. (#3835)

MAN IN THE FLYING LAWN CHAIR
Caroline Cromelin, Eric Nightengale, Monica Read, Kimberly Reiss, Troy W. Taber and Toby Wherry

This high-altitude comedy of errors is based on the true story of Larry Walters, a man who secured his place as a cult hero for weird daredevils everywhere by using surplus weather balloons to launch himself to 16,000 feet in an aluminum lawn chair—and lived to tell about it. Developed through improvisation at the 78th Street Theatre Lab, this winner of the Edinburgh Festival's Best of the Fringe was aired on the BBC. 2 m., 3 f. (#14804)

**Send for your copy of the Samuel French
BASIC CATALOGUE OF PLAYS AND MUSICALS**